MAKE COLOUR WORK FOR YOU

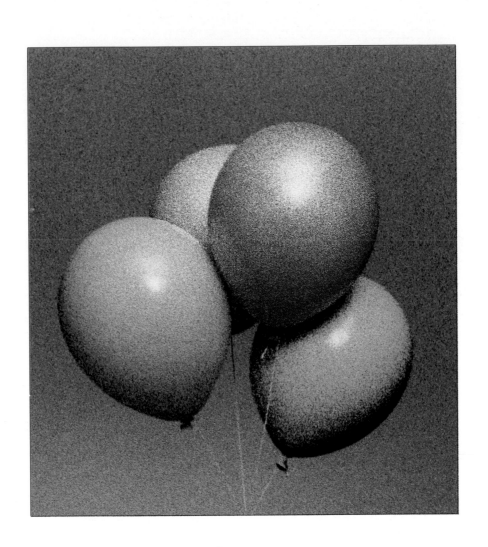

MAKE
COLOUR WORK
FOR YOU

Published by Time-Life Books in association with Kodak

MAKE COLOUR WORK FOR YOU

Created and designed by Mitchell Beazley International
in association with Kodak and TIME-LIFE BOOKS

Editor-in-Chief
Jack Tresidder

Series Editor
John Roberts

Art Editor
Mel Petersen

Editors
Ian Chilvers
Louise Earwaker
Lucy Lidell
Richard Platt

Designers
Robert Lamb
Lisa Tai

Picture Researchers
Brigitte Arora
Nicky Hughes

Editorial Assistant
Margaret Little

Production
Jean Phillips
Jean Rigby

Consulting Photography
Michael Freeman

Coordinating Editors for Kodak
Kenneth Lassiter
Kenneth Obérg
Jacalyn Salitan

Contents

THE MAGIC OF COLOUR

Colours can be breathtaking when their impact is concentrated within the frame of a photograph — deep and resonant reds, subtly modulated greens, singing yellows, solemn or brilliant blues. Although the foundations and traditions of photography were laid in black and white, few photographers today can resist the power of colour to evoke excitement, impact, variety — and simply to delight the eye.

There is, of course, a whole range of photographs in which colour may be no more than an incidental element, subsidiary to the main point — which may be to record an event, or an aspect of human behaviour, or the expression on a single face. However, this book explores something different — the way you can make colour itself the subject of the picture by using it purposefully rather than incidentally. Developing this ability to use colour creatively can be an absorbing adventure, which may change your whole attitude to colour and make you aware that its influence is emotional as well as visual. Colour has its own eloquence. The pictures on the following eleven pages work as they do because colour is the essential element. Imagine, as you turn the pages, how much would be lost if the images were in black and white. This is the magic of colour.

Autumn colours billow in a soft wave over the little girl playing in a park. The picture's charm stems largely from the photographer's decision to allow the beauty of the tree's colours to fill most of the frame.

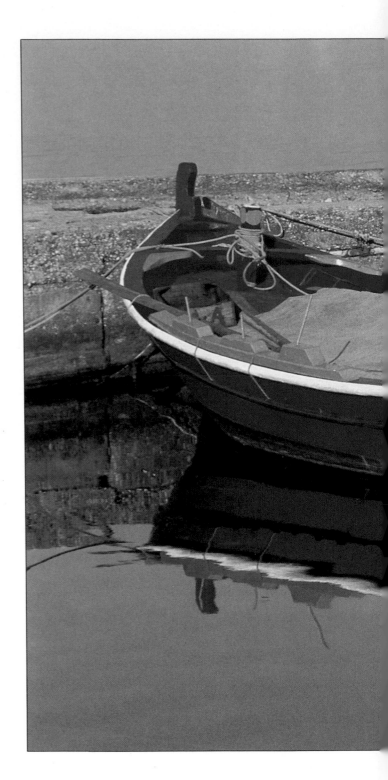

Red boat, blue water, *join in a curve of richly saturated colour. Such images speak to us simply. The photographer needed only to spot the freshly painted boat and frame it closely to relate the strong red to the blue of the sky reflected in the clear water.*

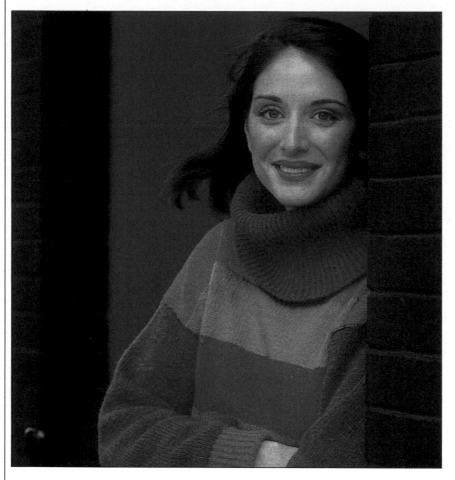

The beauty of a woman,
*her smile, and her patterned
sweater are brought out by
a setting that reveals the
photographer's eye for the
way colours work together.
The vivid red background
and the frame of dark bricks
complement perfectly the
subtle hues of the sweater.*

Pale balloons *float against a sombre background of shadowed architecture in a composition that deliberately restricts colour to a small area of the frame. The surprising impact of the picture demonstrates the power of colour to sway us with the lightest touch.*

Interlocking segments *of solid colour turn a hillside into an abstract pattern that suggests the strength of the landscape itself. The picture has been carefully exposed and printed to heighten the contrasting tones of the sky and hill against the thin yellow line of crops.*

Lily pads, *curving grasses, and the glassy surface of a pond create cool colour harmonies that only an observant eye might notice. By moving in close, you can often discover such hidden beauty in nature and isolate it in pictures.*

Beach umbrellas, *abandoned during a rain shower, sweep in a delicate green arc across the whole picture. The blending and softening of hues on a misty day such as this often creates marvellous opportunities for colour photographs.*

Windblown barley has been blurred here by the choice of a shutter speed too slow to stop the tips of the stalks waving. By this means the photographer has subtly muted the overall colour to pale green.

A motorcycle racer banks over to take a corner, the bright red of the rider's suit standing out against the dark of the track. The photographer used a special prism filter to create the repeated image that gives such a dramatic impression of high speed.

COLOUR AND COLOUR FILMS

One of the most fascinating things about colour photography is the enormous range of colour effects that can appear in your pictures. Very often, colours do not turn out the way you expected – they may be stronger or duller than you remembered them, or there may be an overall tinge of a single colour, of which you were not aware when you took the picture. However, this unpredictable quality is not really so surprising: colour photography involves a delicate relationship between the colours of objects, the colours of light, and those of colour films.

The section that follows begins by looking at the source of all colours – light itself. Because direct sunlight at midday combines all the colours of the spectrum, the illumination it provides may appear colourless. But other light sources, such as light bulbs – and sunlight itself at evening or in the morning – have a definite bias toward orange or red. A person's face can look quite a different colour depending on the quality of the prevailing light. Films are highly sensitive to these colour differences. Moreover, various types and brands of films differ in the emphasis they give to some colours at the expense of others.

To achieve the best results in colour photography, you need to make sure you are using the film most suited to the type of lighting. A few slide films are designed specially for use in the orange light of tungsten studio lamps. Alternatively, you may be able to modify the light passing through the lens by using a filter. The ability to control precisely the colours that appear in your pictures is the first step toward using colour creatively.

A rainbow in the fine spray falling from an overhead fire hose reveals the colours making up the sunlight flooding a Pittsburgh street scene. Although the colours of light are seldom seen so clearly, everything in the world owes its colour to the light that illuminates it.

Light and colour vision

To understand why we see the world in a variety of colours, you need first of all to look at the nature of light itself. Like X-rays or radio waves, light is one of the forms of electromagnetic energy that radiates in waves from energy sources such as the sun – somewhat as rings spread out from a pebble thrown into a pond. The essential difference between the light falling on this page and the signals picked up by a radio or television set is one of wavelength – the distance from the crest of one wave to the crest of the next. In some forms of energy the wavelength is infinitesimal – no more than a billionth of a milli-

metre; in others it can be as much as ten kilometres. The wavelengths of visible light are around 1/2000th of a millimetre.

For the photographer, the important difference between light and any other form of radiant energy is the fact that we can see it. Out of all the wavelengths of energy radiating through the atmosphere, the nerve endings in our eyes are sensitive to only a narrow band that constitutes the visible spectrum, diagrammed below. The ultraviolet and infra-red wavelengths on either side of this band are invisible to our eyes. The eye and the brain assign different

How we perceive the colours of light

The large diagram below graphically simplifies a complex process by which we see colours in the light radiating from the sun. Light itself forms only a tiny band of wavelengths among other forms of energy spreading out in intermingled waves of widely differing lengths. Yet the relatively narrow band of visible wavelengths provides our whole multicoloured world of light. When a prism splits light into its individual wavelengths we can see a spectrum of colours, as in the photograph at right. And, remarkably, we see this by interpreting signals from just three types of cells in the retina, sensitive to wavelengths of red, green or blue light, enabling us to perceive a myriad different hues.

The sun

Gamma rays

X-rays

Ultraviolet
Visible light

Infrared

Microwave

Radio

Prism

Wavelengths of radiant energy vary in frequency according to whether the energy is high, as in gamma and X-rays, or low, as in the long radio waves. Light is simply another form of energy, of medium wavelength.

Fractional differences in wavelengths distinguish the colours of the spectrum. Dividing the spectrum into seven colours is merely a convention – in fact it is a continuous band, made up of numberless hues.

hues to those wavelengths to which they are sensitive, interpreting the longest of them as red and the shortest as violet. In daylight, the wavelengths that make up the visible spectrum are complete, mixing together in such a way that the light appears white, or colourless. But a rainbow reveals the fact that the light actually contains all the spectrum colours, because the droplets of water break apart the individual hues. You can separate the colours of the spectrum simply by passing a beam of white light through a prism, as shown below. And by using a filter to take out one or more of the colours, you can make the light itself look coloured rather than white. For example, a blue filter absorbs red and green lightwaves, allowing only blue to pass.

The reason that we see the world in a multitude of colours is mainly because different substances and surfaces absorb certain wavelengths of light and reflect others back to the eye. The eye then reads the reflected light in terms of the predominant wavelengths, and assigns a hue to it. Thus a tree looks green and a poppy red because they absorb and reflect different wavelengths of the light that shines on them both.

Soap bubbles, like the prism, bring out the colours in white light (right). The surface of a bubble varies in thickness and passes or reflects different colours of light accordingly. The result is a shimmering pattern of shifting colours.

Shorter waves

Longer waves

Why objects look coloured
When rays of light fall on a surface, wavelengths of some colours are absorbed, others reflected. Those reflected back to the eye determine how we perceive an object's colour (below).

Here the ball looks red because only wavelengths we perceive as red are reflected: all the other wavelengths are absorbed.

When wavelengths of more than one primary colour are reflected back (such as red and green), they create a new colour (here, brown).

If an object reflects all the spectrum's wavelengths and absorbs none, it will appear to be coloured white, as does this ball.

Both the eye and colour film respond to light in terms of three predominant colour wavelengths – red, green and blue. But the varying mixtures of these colours mean that we can perceive countless gradations of hue.

The balance of colour/1

The sun, a candle and a glowing coal all give off light as they release heat. But the colour of the light that each produces is not identical, because the heat at which each source burns varies enormously. As a result, each source sends out a different mixture of wavelengths, with substantial effects on the colours of the objects illuminated. These effects are particularly noticeable in colour photographs because films are balanced to give accurate colours in light of a particular wavelength mixture.

There is no point in relying on your eyes to detect minor changes in lighting. We see what we expect to see, ignoring subtle variations of colour. A white shirt will still look white to us whether we see it in sunlight or indoors under artificial light. However, film records the predominant colour of the lighting literally. Ordinary film for daylight use is balanced for average noon light in which the illumination comes mainly from the predominantly white light of the direct sun. Unless you correct it with a filter, lighting of a very different balance will inevitably change the colours in photographs taken with this same film, producing unreal colours – an effect known as a colour cast.

The colour of a light source does not depend only on its heat. For example, atmospheric factors come into play when we consider the way daylight changes in colour. As a result, whereas daylight or noon sun appears neutral, the wavelength mixture reaching us varies as the sun rises or sets. Similarly, clouds or haze filter out some wavelengths by absorption, or scatter others so that they predominate in the light reflected from the sky itself. On a clear day, the sky looks intensely blue because of the scattering of blue wavelengths by atmospheric molecules. And this means that the light is much bluer in shaded areas, where illumination comes only from the sky, than in areas reached by the light of direct sun.

Light sources can be codified according to their so-called colour temperature on the kelvin (k) scale. Temperature is the mode of measurement because a heated object, such as an iron bar, will change colour from red through yellow and white to dazzling blue as the temperature increases. But remember that the kelvin number assigned to a light source relates to the colour of the light produced, not to the physical heat of the source. Thus, the colour temperature of daylight may be higher (because bluer) on a cold overcast day when all the light is coming from the sky, than in direct warm sun. At midday, average (photographic) daylight has a colour temperature of about 5,500k, and it is for light of this colour temperature that most colour films are balanced.

The colour temperature scale
Whether you are photographing in artificial or natural light, all light sources have a certain preponderance of wavelengths that give the lighting a particular colour. These different colours are shown below as a band of rising colour temperatures, extending from the reddish lighting characteristic of candlelight and sunsets up to the bluer light normally found in pictures taken in the shade or on overcast days. The colour effects of natural light in various conditions are illustrated above the colour temperature band, those of artificial light sources below the band.

Candles
Oil lamps

Household
lightbulbs

Sunrise or
sunset

2,000k

Candlelight, in the absence of any other light source, produces a strong reddish-yellow cast, because a candle burns at a far lower temperature than the noonday sun. Although the light is usually too dim to show much detail, pictures taken by this source can have strong atmosphere, as in this shot of a Bangkok procession.

At sunrise and sunset, natural light is at its reddest because the light has to travel farther through the atmosphere. As a result, many short blue wavelengths are absorbed, allowing the longer red wavelengths to predominate. Below, the sunset sky has tinged the grey rocks of the Grand Canyon with red light.

At noon, with a few white clouds, daylight is neutral in colour. Because this is the light for which most films are balanced, the colours of objects under noon sunlight look correct. The picture of kites on a beach was taken in these conditions – and shows pure whites and reds in the nearest kite.

In the shade, photographs often have a strong blue cast, because objects are illuminated only by light reflected from the blue sky, and receive no direct sunlight. Overcast skies also usually produce bluish colours. Here, a cool blue light suffuses both the white ibis and the water.

Morning or evening sunlight		Average noon daylight Electronic flash		Hazy sky	Heavily overcast sky	Reflection from clear blue sky (shade)

5,500k   16,000k

Household bulbs burn hotter than candles, but produce a much yellower light than does the sun. This means that with ordinary daylight film in the camera, pictures taken in room lighting usually have an overall orange cast. The picture of a sleeping child shows that the warm effect of this light can suit skin tones.

Electronic flash is balanced to match the colour temperature of noon daylight. Thus, you can use it safely indoors or out, without creating colour casts. Had this studio flash portrait been taken by the light of tungsten photographic lamps, a special slide film (described overleaf) would have been needed.

Fluorescent light
This does not belong on the colour temperature scale because it is not a burning light source. The colour casts it produces vary greatly. Above, the greenish lights of an airport runway give the Concorde a surreal look.

The balance of colour/2

Not many situations in photography call for any special measures to cope with the colour quality of the light. Most pictures are taken outdoors by the light of the sky or sun, and slight variations in colour caused by weather conditions or time of day often add pictorial interest rather than cause problems (see pages 56-84). But sometimes a light source produces a colour mixture too far removed from the lighting for which your film is intended. When this happens, unacceptable colour casts may appear in the picture – for example, green flesh tones in a portrait. You can avoid this situation either by choosing special film or by using filters to modify the light as it enters the lens. Colour print films have a fair tolerance to different kinds of light because corrections can be made in processing, but with slide film the balance is crucial.

A special slide film is available for shooting indoors under tungsten bulbs. However, this film is balanced for powerful lamps used in photography studios, and will not entirely remove the unnatural colour cast produced by ordinary, lower-wattage bulbs. Alternatively, conversion and light-balancing filters are available in a complete range of colours, including those for fluorescent lighting. Some of the most useful filters are demonstrated here.

Daylight and film balance
Most colour films, print and slide, are designed to work best in daylight, accurately reproducing the colours we see (right). Almost all the film you use will be balanced for daylight. The exception is slide film balanced for tungsten lighting. This film has a bluer quality overall, rendering a scene lit by orange light from tungsten lamps as near white. Used in ordinary daylight, the film produces unnatural blues (far right).

1 – Daylight with daylight film

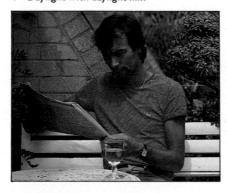

2 – with tungsten film

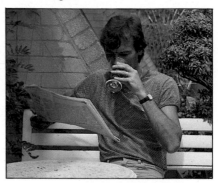

Tungsten light and film balance
In tungsten light, whether from ordinary bulbs or special tungsten photographic lamps, film balanced for daylight records an orange or yellow cast (right). Although the warm colour can be attractive, this is not how we see the scene. For more accurate results, the light can be partly corrected with a bluish No. 80A filter (far right, above). However, for greater accuracy, use slide film balanced for tungsten light (far right, below).

1 – Tungsten light with daylight film

2 – with No. 80A filter

3 – with tungsten film

Filtering fluorescent light

Although fluorescent lamps look white to the eye, they produce an unpredictable variety of colour casts on film – ranging through yellow, blue or green. The scene in an airport control tower at right has a distinctly greenish cast from the fluorescent tubes. A fluorescent filter (far right) does not balance the light perfectly to the daylight film, but does give a warmer, more natural look.

1 – Fluorescent light with daylight film

2 – with fluorescent filter

Filtering overcast daylight

Heavy clouds scatter the shorter blue wavelengths of sunlight, raising the colour temperature of the light and producing a blue cast on film (right). This still-life was rephotographed with a No. 81B pink filter to reduce the proportion of blue (far right). Many photographers use this filter as a matter of course on cloudy days.

1 – Overcast daylight with daylight film

2 – with No. 81B filter

Corrective printing: tungsten light

Filtration control in printing may restore accurate colours to print film. The portrait photographed in household tungsten light (right) has a strong orange cast. By asking the printer for a reprint with corrective filtration (far right), the photographer secured a much more accurate result.

1 – Tungsten light, uncorrected

2 – with corrective printing

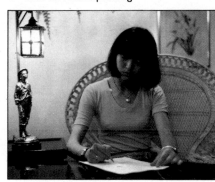

Corrective printing: fluorescent light

The green cast from fluorescent light is more obtrusive than the orange from tungsten lamps. This portrait, shot by the light from fluorescent tubes in an office (right), has an unpleasant colour if uncorrected. When asked to compensate, the printer produced an improvement (far right), but has not succeeded in imitating the natural colours of a daylit scene.

1 – Fluorescent light, uncorrected

2 – with corrective printing

Choosing colour film

Most photographers simply want the film they use to record accurately the colours they see. Thus it may seem surprising that such a range of colour film is available. For 35mm cameras, there are several dozen types of daylight and indoor films. The reason for this diversity is that each film has its own characteristics, and you may want to choose different films for different purposes.

The initial choice, of course, lies between films for slides (transparencies) or for negatives from which you can make prints. Beyond this, a film's sensitivity to light is the main consideration. Fast films are very sensitive, and give the photographer great versatility, but slower, less sensitive films have other advantages. For example, they provide a good range of tones between light and dark. And because they make use of finer grains of light-sensitive silver salts to form an image, they can look sharper and are less grainy in big enlargements than photographs taken on faster film.

Although grain size is a consideration when choosing colour film, the film's colour rendition is often more important. A photograph of the same scene taken on different types of film will vary slightly but distinctly in colour, as the pictures below show. One film may record reds with special intensity. Another may distinguish more clearly colours that are closely similar. Yet another film may give the picture a warmer or cooler appearance overall – this is particularly noticeable in neutral colour areas such as black, white and grey, and in skin tones. In photographs, it is often in the skin tones that we are most sensitive to variations in colour values and most disturbed by unnaturalness.

Variations of colour are usually quite subtle, and are most obvious when you make comparisons between slide films; the printing process tends to reduce the differences between negative films. In general, photographers form their own preferences for colour film. The best way to make a choice is to try out a number of films, and decide which you like most. You may even want to use two different films, choosing for portraits a type that produces very natural skin tones, but preferring a different film for landscapes, where you may feel that the rendition of blues and greens is more important. The difference in the qualities of the blues is one of the features of the colour films shown below.

The colour characteristics of film
This garden still-life incorporates a
wide range of colours. Shot on different
types of film, the colours show slight
but distinct differences – for example,
in some the blue is stronger, in others
the red. The green is particularly strong
in the image second from right. However,
there is no "best," because colour
judgments are largely subjective.

Subtle colours and flowing movement emphasize the grace and beauty of dance. Here, the photographer chose high-speed film to cope with the dim light of the rehearsal room. This film has helped to soften the colours.

A vivid piece of woven fabric relies for its impact on the juxtaposition of primary colours. The photographer took the picture with slow transparency film, which has moderate contrast and good colour fidelity, suited to the reproduction of vibrant hues.

How colour film works

Colour print film is like a layer cake (above) made of gelatin containing grains of silver salts. Each layer records a different part of the visible spectrum – red, green or blue light. Processing creates a silver image where light was absorbed in each layer. At the same time, a dye image appears – in colour exactly opposite to the colour for which the layer is sensitized. For example, the blue-sensitive layer forms a yellow dye image. After bleach and fix have removed the silver image, the dye layers (visible in the magnified cross-section above) form the negative from which a positive print is made. Processing of colour slides is more complex because the film must form a positive picture. During processing, a second development introduces transparent dyes that form the image, subtracting appropriate colours from the light that passes through the slide.

Slide film

To achieve precision and brilliance of colour, many photographers prefer to use colour slide film – often called transparency or colour reversal film. Because this produces a positive film image directly, without an intermediate printing process, any adjustment the photographer makes to the camera's controls leads directly to a corresponding change in the appearance of the final picture.

Although colour slides need projection or enlargement to be seen properly, they display great brilliance and colour saturation. We see slides by transmitted, rather than reflected, light. Therefore, the range of brightness is higher – a slide usually has more snap than a print (see overleaf).

This impact derives partly from the higher contrast of slide films – they allow little latitude for over- or underexposure. On a dull day, or under flat lighting, this is an advantage, but on a bright sunny day, when the shadows are very dark and the highlights bright, high contrast can prove a problem. At worst you can lose highlight or shadow detail altogether, depending on how you set the exposure.

As a general rule, blank highlights – for example pale, washed-out features in a portrait – are more likely to spoil a picture than are murky shadows. For this reason, if you are uncertain about the light, some underexposure of colour slide film is better than overexposure.

Regular users of colour transparency film often deliberately underexpose all their pictures to take account of this – usually by a third or half a stop. Even in low or flat lighting conditions, slight underexposure leads to richer, more saturated colours. You can also underexpose by setting your camera's film speed control to a slightly higher speed – say ISO 80 if you are using ISO 64 film.

When the contrast between highlights and shadows is very high – in strong sunlight or when shooting into the sun – bracketing exposures increases the chance of getting just the picture you want. For the sunset pictures shown below, the photographer used this simple technique, making exposures at intervals of one stop above and below the setting indicated by the camera's meter.

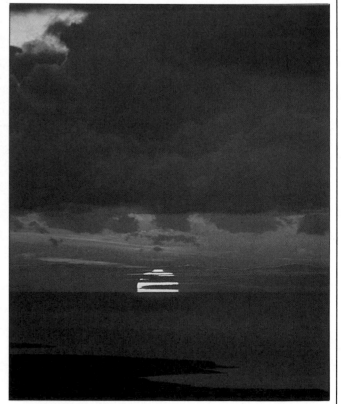

The sunset looks different in this picture than in the three on the right, because the photographer varied or bracketed the exposure so that he could choose the best. The image above received two stops more exposure than the meter indicated. The result is pale but pleasing, with a satisfying balance of tones.

One stop overexposure gives the best balanced result. There is more detail in the sand spit and clouds compared with the pictures on the right.

Underexposure of colour slide film can add to colour saturation and avoid the burned-out appearance of sunlit highlights. For the picture of a flower bed (right), the photographer deliberately set the camera to give half a stop less exposure than the meter indicated. The inset shows the "correct" exposure setting (above).

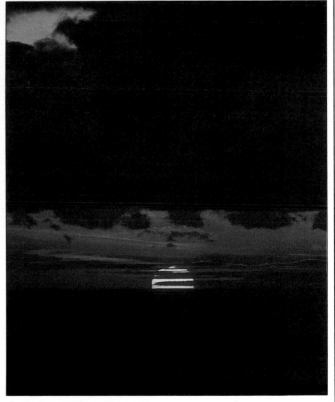

At the metered setting, most of the cloud and sea areas are left as broad masses, but in compensation the red sky is particularly rich.

One stop underexposure produces an image that loses almost all the detail, but is still acceptable because of its dramatic effect.

Print film

While slide films have the advantage of brilliance and colour intensity, you need to project them onto a screen or use a small viewer to see them at their best. Many people prefer to see their pictures in the form of a print which they can hold in their hands. And because of the brilliance of the original, a paper print made from a transparency rarely seems as satisfactory. If your principal aim is prints, then colour negative film may be your best choice.

Because a print is viewed in different conditions to a slide, its colours may appear more muted, and some photographers prefer to work with colour negative film because they consider that the hues and tones of a print have more subtlety than those of a slide. Another significant difference is the low contrast of a negative compared with a slide. If you hold a negative up to the light it will look relatively dull. However, because the negative is only an intermediate step on the way to a print, low contrast is not the disadvantage it may seem. It means that negative film can be corrected for some over- or underexposure. As a result the film is ideal for simple cameras that do not have sophisticated ways of avoiding exposure errors. Even when loaded into an SLR camera, negative film needs less care in assessing exposure than does slide film because to a certain extent exposure errors can be corrected during printing.

Printing a colour negative can be much more than just the mechanical process of reversing colours to their normal hues. First, a colour-correcting mask that gives the negative an orange tint has to be removed. Then, and more significantly, printing provides the opportunity to control selectively the overall or local colour of the picture, and to correct for errors in colour balance as well as exposure.

For the many photographers who print their own negatives in home darkrooms, the printing process can, in fact, be just as creative as actually taking photographs. Even if you do not have a home darkroom, you can exert some measure of control over the appearance of the final print by examining a contact sheet (see opposite) and giving appropriate directions to the colour laboratory.

The unreal hues of a colour negative (right) are little help in judging the final colour of the print (above). Part of the problem is the orange dye mask that covers the whole of the negative. This helps to produce more accurate colours in the print, but makes interpretation of the reversed colours more difficult. The best general guide to how a negative will print is its density. A thin negative – one that is underexposed – has little visible detail and will produce a dark, muddy print. By comparison, a dense negative – one that is overexposed – creates fewer problems for the printer.

Purple in the negative will appear as yellow in the print – the orange mask has combined with blue (the complementary of yellow) to give the purple appearance.

Yellow in the negative also forms its complementary colour – blue – on the print. The orange mask distorts yellow only slightly.

Green in the negative will print as red – the gloves in the girl's pocket.

A contact sheet, on which an entire roll of film has been printed, provides you with a convenient working guide to the appearance of all the pictures on the roll. Most laboratories can make a contact sheet, from which you can then choose which images to enlarge, say how they should be cropped to improve the composition, and decide if colour correction is needed. From this roll, the photographer picked out the image of the boat, and asked the printer to bring out the overall warm colour and crop the picture on the left-hand side. Both these changes would be simple to make in a home darkroom.

31

Instant-picture film

The obvious and spectacular advantage of an instant-picture camera is that it provides a finished print almost immediately. But apart from this fundamental attribute, an instant picture has a certain unique and identifiable quality – because the film reproduces colours by a method different from that used for any other type of film.

The elaborate chemistry of instant-picture film effectively packs a mini-darkroom into the sheet of film itself. Once development is complete, the image you see is the same size as the image recorded on the film, so that no quality is lost by enlargement. However, because the plastic-wrapped sandwich of film has to act as the print as well, the final image lacks some of the fineness of detail that can be achieved with conventional film. At the same time, the sealing of the actual print surface produces a slight diffusion of the colours. The combination of these two qualities gives the instant image its unique look. You will find that some subjects are actually flattered by the characteristic tonal and colour qualities of instant-picture prints.

In general, instant-picture film will give best results when the light is not too bright and contrasty, so that you can avoid the danger of colours being lost in inky shadows or pale highlights. The richness of the colours on the page opposite shows what can be achieved in more even lighting. Many of the newer instant-picture cameras reduce the problem of high contrast by providing automatic flash to lighten dense shadow areas caused by particularly bright sunlight.

One of the great attractions of instant-picture photography is that you can take advantage of the immediacy of the process by assessing results on the spot and using them as the basis for improvements. For example, the picture below was the best of several attempts to produce an image in which the moving ball stayed within the frame. In this sense, an instant-picture camera can be an invaluable tool for learning how to compose better pictures. No other kind of photography enables you to see so quickly and clearly how a three-dimensional scene will translate into a flat image.

The boy kicking a ball was the best of several shots. Because the photographer could see the results within a few seconds, he was able to take more pictures until he got the precise effect he desired, with the soccer ball included in the frame. The image appears sharp at the end of a trail of movement because the automatic flash of the camera fired to give extra light while the shutter was open. This froze part of the movement.

Instant pictures make an ideal visual notebook (right). On holiday, you can use them to make personal "wish you were here" messages to send to friends.

COMPOSING WITH COLOUR

Colour does more than bring photographs closer to reality. Particular colours often provoke strong responses in the viewer, creating tension or excitement, establishing a soothing feeling of equilibrium or jarring the senses. These powerful reactions may be independent of the subject of the picture, for we react to colour emotionally.

Controlling the strength or placement of colours can enable you to produce more effective colour pictures. On a few occasions you will have the opportunity to alter the colours of the subject – you could, for example, ask someone to wear a particular colour for a portrait, or change the colour of a backcloth. Much more easily, you can manipulate the colours that actually appear in the image by using techniques of composition outlined in the section that follows. For example, you can choose a viewpoint or a lens to include certain areas of colour and exclude others. You can fill the viewfinder frame with vivid hues, as in the picture here, or restrict bright colour to just a small area. And you can juxtapose two or more colours for either a calming or a vigorous effect. Colours create mood, and by using them in a controlled way you can give pictures just the impact or subtlety you want.

A sea of colour, created by the heads of innumerable wild flowers, sets up a lively and joyous mood. In this picture, close framing has concentrated attention on the interplay of the two colours, rather than the topographical details of the landscape.

Colour psychology

Individual responses to colour are highly subjective. But although most of us feel – rather than think – about colours, effective photographs often come from understanding the basic factors that influence people's reactions to colour.

Some reactions have a physiological basis. For example, yellow strikes us as lively partly because the cells of the retina are especially sensitive to yellow-green wavelengths of light. Some colour combinations appear vibrant because in looking at them our eyes have to make rapid adjustments between different wavelengths, whereas combinations of colours closer in wavelengths appear harmonious and restful. Again, bright, vivid colours – such as the red of the leaves in the picture at right – tend to seem nearer than do more muted hues.

More often, however, psychological factors are at work. These may arise from personal experiences, leading us to develop preferences for certain colours in clothes or furnishings. However, in learning how to use colour in photography, such personal reactions are less relevant than other responses to colour that are very widely shared – for example, the sense of warmth or coolness. Reds and oranges commonly seem to have an actual physical warmth, perhaps by association with fire and sun, whereas blue, by association with water, shade and dawn, seems cool. Another widespread feeling is that some colours are softer than others – pastel hues, such as pinks and pale greens, appear more delicate and gentle than pure, intense colours, such as yellows and reds, which can seem dramatic, strident, or even aggressive. By understanding such general reactions to colour, and by using one combination rather than another, you can consciously create a whole range of emotional effects.

Unbroken bands of cool blue *convey a sense of peace and tranquillity. The atmosphere evoked by colours depends not only on their hue and brightness but also on how they are arranged – horizontal lines are much calmer in feeling than vertical or diagonal lines.*

Bright red leaves seem almost to leap from the page in this vivid image. Whereas bright, warm colours advance toward us, cooler, darker colours appear to recede. Here the muted background emphasizes the vibrancy of the leaves.

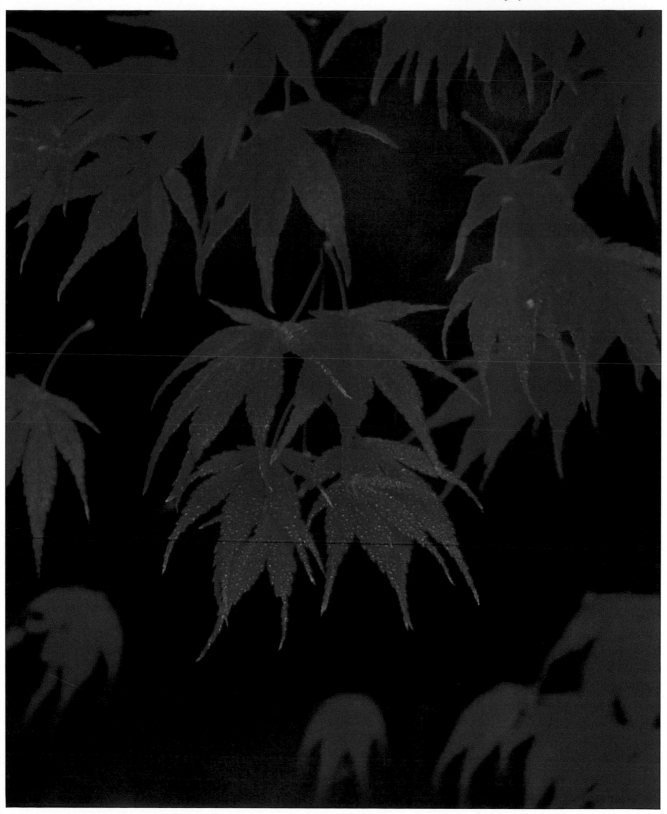

The richness of colour

Strong colours have a more direct impact than those that are muted. Of course, many good photographs have soft colours, for these subtler hues often contribute to the sense of balance or atmosphere in a shot. But when you want colours to contribute drama or have a vigorous effect, you usually want them to appear at their most vivid.

The strongest colours are said to be fully "saturated" – a term borrowed from the dyeing industry. In photography, saturated colours are those that consist of one or two of the primary colours of light – red, green or blue – but not all three, because that introduces an element of greyness. At the same time the saturated colours look most vivid in a certain kind of lighting. For example, a pure red flower will appear more vivid than one that has a brownish tinge, but both will appear most colourful in light of medium intensity. Bright sunlight can make a colour

appear less vivid by lightening it – as the left-hand picture of the leaves below demonstrates. Shade, on the other hand, can make the colours appear darker.

When you have identified an area of colour that you want to emphasize, the following techniques may help you take full advantage of its richness. First, consider whether you can move around until the angle at which light strikes the subject brings out the strongest colour. Unless the subject reflects glare, a position with the sun behind the camera will usually be best. Second, to reproduce the colour at maximum saturation, take the exposure reading from the chosen part of the scene rather than the whole view. Although this may underexpose duller parts of the subject, the contrast can enhance the chosen colour area. Finally, with slide film, deliberately underexposing by a half-stop tends to enrich colour, as well as producing good shadow detail.

1 – Glare reflecting from a shiny bush (above) gives the entire photograph a washed-out appearance. The other two pictures were taken in the same light, showing that colour saturation in direct sunlight depends on the lighting angle.

2 – Backlighting, with the bush between camera and sun, gives dramatic contrast in which the leaves are very bright. But because the light shining through the leaves is too strong, the colours appear somewhat washed-out.

3 – Bright light without glare shows fully saturated leaves. The photographer took up a position different from the first two, altering the angle between sun, subject and camera. Slight underexposure increases the richly coloured effect.

Colour saturation
Pure colours lose intensity if they are either darkened or lightened. The saturated hues at the centre of the diagram are progressively desaturated by the addition of white or black. In photography, this means that colours lose strength in shade, or as light glares from a surface. Exposure errors also make colours look less vivid.

Low light mutes even the pure colours of these flowering trees, an effect that is increased by the haze. The green foliage is so dulled that it is almost grey in colour. In conditions such as these, only the strongest colours, perfectly exposed, will preserve any intensity.

Perfectly lit by soft window light, a bowl of fruit shows the richness of fully saturated colours. But even here, the effect of light reflecting from the subject can be seen in the highlights on the green apples. With slightly more exposure, these areas would have begun to appear too light and washed-out.

The colour accent

Colourful scenes make naturally colourful pictures, but much of our environment – particularly the concrete wasteland of modern cities – is drab. The weather, too, can have a profound effect on colour: snow blankets everything in purest white, and a scene that glows with colour in sunlight can look grey and forbidding in drizzle. Occasionally, a picture made up simply of subtle shades of grey has a quiet, pearly beauty of its own (see pages 44-45), but more often, a colourless scene looks simply dull.

Yet by introducing a single patch of colour into just such a picture, you can make the image pulse with energy, as in the picture of a dockside at top right. Even a small accent is enough to make a difference. For example, the graveyard on the oppo-site page looks drab and depressing if you cover the flowers in the picture with your finger. But with the splash of yellow in the foreground, the picture springs to life as a harmonious image. The warmth of the yellow draws attention to other, more subtle patches of muted colour – the moss on the tomb-stones, for example.

The colours that best provide sharp accents are the warm ones – reds, yellows and fiery oranges. These colours jump out from the picture surface and command the viewer's attention. Cooler colours, such as blues and greens, often are less effective. Unless they are very bright and luminous, you may need to use them more liberally if you want to enliven a predominantly grey picture.

A fishing dock stands empty and silent as storm clouds sweep in from the sea. The heavily overcast sky had drained the sea of colour – but intensified the bright pink of a buoy – so the photographer stepped back to include this foreground accent.

Brooklyn Bridge is such a popular subject for New York photographers that presenting an original view is difficult. Yet in the picture at left, the cyclist's red pack provides a brilliant patch of colour that focuses the eye on his route towards the greys, blues and whites of the Manhattan skyline.

Yellow flowers in an improvised vase break up a drab pattern of tombstones. Because the stone slabs look so grey and ponderous, the blooms seem to glow with light and colour – whereas on a florist's stand, their brilliance might be lost among the other competing hues.

The dominant colour

The ability of modern colour film to reproduce all the brilliant colours around us tempts photographers to fill the viewing frame with the richest mixture possible. Sheer profusion of colour sometimes works well, but if you are not careful, the picture becomes a jumble of clashing hues.

Often, you can exploit rich, bright colour more simply by allowing just one powerful hue to dominate the image. Restricting the colour palette in this way can concentrate the impact of the picture – in the startlingly blue seascape shown below, the single block of colour seems more emphatic than would several colours jostling for attention.

This way of using colour often works best when the dominant colour forms a unified background – as does the bright yellow of the umbrella on the right. The more intense the colour, the more it will dominate the image, but paler colour areas can be used to frame areas of the photograph that are a different hue. For example, in the picture on the right, the lemon of the umbrella makes a lively and vivid backdrop for the girl's shy smile.

To make best use of large, commanding areas of colour, try to set them off against other, more neutral, parts of the picture – here the black of the girl's hair, and her white shirt. You may be able to compose the picture so as to exclude discordant, distracting colour in favour of muted hues, such as the soft browns of earth – or of skin itself.

Sea and sky turn deep azure in dawn light.
The dark colour, deliberately underexposed,
emphasizes the lights of the island temple.

*A yellow **umbrella** makes a vibrant background for this simple picture – a delightful rainy-day portrait. The light filtering through the fabric is soft and flattering, warming the whole image, and enhancing the tones of the girl's skin.*

Limited colour

Images that have very little colour at all can some-times be extraordinarily evocative. Such nearly monochromatic pictures are expressive in a much quieter way than are most colour photographs, but they often have a compelling simplicity and beauty. Not least, they draw our attention because they are relatively uncommon.

Two main types of monochromatic images are those in which the lighting or the prevailing weather conditions provide an overall draining or blending of colours, and those in which the subject itself has little variety of colour. A landscape lit by weak sun, early or late in the day, will tend to have a predominant orange glow, especially if there is a haze or dust in the air. Rain, fog, mist, smoke – even pollution in industrial areas – scatter light and mute colours, reducing the colour range of the most variegated subjects. You can sometimes use the glow of a fire or the colour of artificial light to tint a scene with a single, overall colour. One useful tip for enhancing the effect of a coloured light source is to shoot toward it without a lens shade, so that light flaring into the lens spreads the colour over the whole image, often producing attractive effects.

Subjects that are monochromatic in themselves are usually more difficult to find – unless you can take the picture at close range. As a general rule, the larger your subject, the more likely it is to contain a variety of colours. For this reason, a long lens with its narrow field of view is far more useful than is a wide-angle lens for limiting the colour range. Finally, you can always underline the prevailing mood of an existing colour range with a pale coloured filter.

Soft spray, thrown up by the turbulent waters of Victoria Falls, scatters the light, suppressing true colours and rendering the whole scene in a subdued sepia tone. Only the skeleton of the tree stands out against the mist.

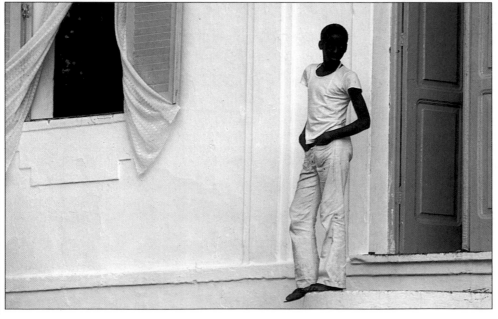

White and black tones can make subtle, effective combinations on colour film. You need to develop your powers of observation to find a picture as simple yet expressive as this one.

The golden sunset sky suffuses the Cape of Good Hope with glowing light. A long lens has compressed distance, bringing closer the silhouetted ships on the horizon.

Ice-blue tones of the grass form a soft backdrop to the dark shape of the horse, photographed in failing light. When using a limited colour range, look for bold shapes to provide contrast.

Colour harmony

Although the way we see colours is highly subjective, most people agree that certain combinations of colours appear more pleasing or harmonious to the eye than others. Moreover, a restricted range of colours makes it easier to create a harmonious composition. A photograph made up of slight variations of a single colour, for example, will obviously convey a sense of harmony. So will a mixture of one main colour with various neutral shades – greys, browns, white or black. Combining two or more colours requires care. As the colour wheel on the right shows, adjacent hues harmonize readily, but opposites contrast strongly. Thus, blues merge well with greens, whereas red and green compete for the viewer's attention, setting up an optical impression of vibrancy.

However, there are exceptions to the general rule. Colours that are adjacent on the wheel may clash if they are very bright – a vivid red combined with a bright magenta, for example. Conversely, strongly contrasting colours can harmonize if their tones are either dark and muted or pale and washed out. For example, in the picture of the beach huts on the opposite page, subdued light has blended together a number of different colours. Think of the way the muted red and golden hues of an autumn landscape blend with the subdued greens. In practice, photographing colours harmoniously is a matter of composing your shots carefully to exclude any colours you judge may detract from the mood of the whole. If the hues appear too strident, you can also try waiting for softer lighting from a low or diffused sun to tone everything down.

Colour wheel
Arrangement of the main colour components of light on a wheel makes it easy to see how different hues work together. Here, the wheel is made up of the three primary colours – red, green and blue – and their complementaries – cyan, magenta and yellow. Half the circle has "cool" colours – green, cyan and blue – and half has "warm" colours – magenta, red and yellow. Colours that are close together on the wheel harmonize. But if tones are made paler, even the most contrasting colours blend – as can be seen here toward the centre of the wheel.

Bright orange berries vary the mosaic of green leaves, but they do not detract from the natural harmony of the yellow and greens. You can include a contrasting colour without disturbing the balance of the whole, if the contrasting area is small enough. Here the photographer stresses patterns of colour as the subject of the picture.

A row of beach huts at dusk creates a darkly harmonious colour composition. In spite of the fairly wide range of colours, the tones are all muted and therefore convey a sense of tranquillity. The cool blue sand in the foreground helps to unify the shot.

Half a lemon, dried out by the sun, rests on a translucent painted plate. Although the lighting is bright and direct, all three of the colours blend together, providing a simple but unusual example of warm colour harmony.

Dramatic colour

Just as some colours look balanced or harmonious when photographed together, others seem to contrast dramatically, and produce a bold, vibrant effect. You can use such dynamic combinations to inject excitement into a picture, to draw attention to a subject, or purely to create a strong abstract impact. Colour contrast is most striking when you restrict your picture to two or three colours – any more than this and the effect will be restless.

The colours likely to produce the most striking contrast are those that lie opposite one another on the colour wheel – the warm reds, yellows and oranges against the cool blues and greens, as in the photographs here. But what really determines how much two colours contrast is their relative brightness. Generally the effect is most dramatic if the two hues are equally bright. Pure colour contrasts are often easier to find on a relatively small scale – by closing in on a shop window display, for example. When you have complete control over the ingredients of your picture, you can consciously set up bold colour contrasts, as the photographer did for the fashion shot on the opposite page.

Ornamental plants often have colours almost as vivid as the artificial dyes and pigments in fabric and paint. At left, richly coloured coleus leaves provide a perfect colour contrast – red and green are opposite each other on the colour wheel.

A delicate green sapling stands out crisply against the bright red fence, below left. The tree's fragility seems underlined by the strength of the red. A powerful yet very simple composition accentuates the dramatic contrast of colours.

A bright blue door makes the girl's yellow trousers look all the more vivid. The photographer has used the blue background to both isolate and frame the figure. And the picture shows how contrast increases when two light hues are juxtaposed.

Restless colour

When a number of rich, bright colours crowd one another in a scene, the effect is usually lively, and the tone of the image upbeat. Such images are unusual in the natural world, because colours there tend to be muted or combine in a generally harmonious way. You are more likely to find bright arrays of clashing colours at carnivals, flower markets, amusement parks, or cities at night – places full of the things we make or display.

Although strong colours in themselves tend to give us pleasure – and we respond immediately to colourful views – photographing such scenes successfully can be surprisingly difficult. The challenge is to capture the vitality without introducing a sense of confusion. Our experience of the scene itself is different from the view of the camera because the eye is selective, and introduces order by concentrating on those elements we find appealing. However, when translated into a photograph, the coloured elements can assume equal importance and appear as a confused jumble. Even worse, the very profusion of colour can make individual hues lose their force.

Because we apply more critical visual interest to a photograph, we expect to find balance or a sense of coherent composition in the way the colours are arranged. To work, compositions with a restless array of colours must be particularly well planned.

The simplest technique for exploiting the vigour of clashing colours is to close in and fill the frame with their richness – as in the pictures here of a pile of plastic cups and a carpet of brilliant autumn leaves. Moving in is also a useful technique for organizing the picture when a situation bursts with life and movement – as might a carnival procession, for example. Multicoloured close-ups often provide a better sense of the excitement of the occasion than could a longer view. Try using a wide-angle lens.

Another way of achieving selection by framing closely is to use a telephoto lens from a greater distance. Do not be afraid to cut off parts of bodies or other elements with the edge of the frame. The lively night picture at the foot of the opposite page shows that you need only to concentrate on the pattern made by the colours in the viewfinder.

Plastic cups piled in a heap become almost overpowering when framed tightly to exclude the surroundings. Such synthetic colours often make brash, eye-catching images when seen together.

Fallen leaves form a pattern of russets, golds and reds. The colours of autumn sometimes seem subtle on the trees, but by raking them together and arranging them for the camera, the photographer exaggerated the contrasts and was able to produce an image with stronger colour opposites than those usually found in nature.

City lights jutting against the deep blue of the night sky here produce an exciting combination. The choice of an aggressive upward view contrasts the red and green of the traffic signals with the yellow of the floodlit church behind.

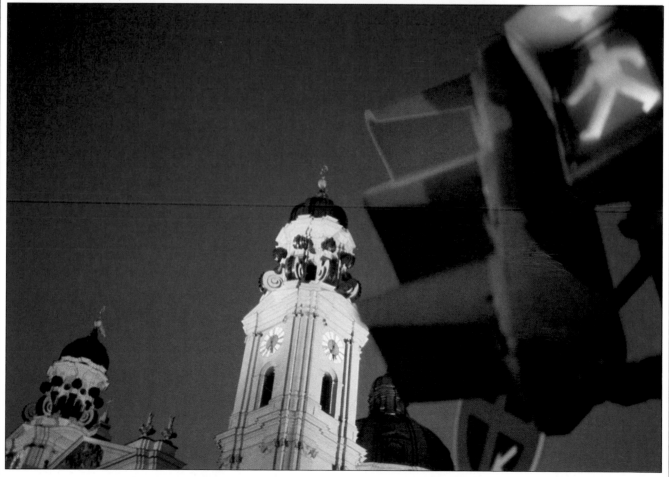

Using coloured foregrounds

To use colour creatively, you need to be able not only to choose colours that will work well together but also to control the position they occupy within the picture. Sometimes, a simple way of strengthening a composition is to use bold colour in the foreground. If the balance is right, this can act as a kind of frame for the scene beyond, leading the viewer's eye into the rest of the picture and perhaps establishing a colour key for the whole image.

Pure, bright colours create the most arresting effects. But you run the risk of overwhelming the rest of the picture if the foreground elements are too strong and sharply detailed. In the picture on the opposite page, the photographer overcame this problem by using a close viewpoint and a wide aperture to keep the bright lengths of material out of focus. When you want to retain detail in a coloured foreground, make sure that the area really strengthens the picture and does not prevent the viewer noticing important background elements. Compose the shots so that the proportions of colours, or their alignment, balance the composition, as in the pictures near right and below.

Colourful canvas stripes almost fill the whole frame, yet their receding lines lead us back to the hang-gliders in the distance. The photographer got down low to shoot across the wings of a grounded glider.

Shades of blue (below) link foreground and background in a picture that celebrates the power of pure colour. The crane, tilting in the opposite direction to the bar of the red sign, just balances the foreground.

Vivid bands of cloth hung to dry enliven this picture, even though they are out of focus. The eye hurdles them and passes on to the smiling face of the woman. The bold strength of the foreground colour balances the bright blue material in the background and together the two colour areas serve to frame the head – the only element in the picture that is in focus.

Using coloured backgrounds

Another important means of controlling colour combinations in photography is by carefully selecting the background. Provided the background does not swamp the subject but sets it off to advantage, you can often allow an intense colour to fill much of the frame. The subject itself will be emphasized if you choose a background that forms a strong contrast – a neutral tone for a brightly coloured subject, a vivid background for a more monochromatic one such as the limousine below. If you have total control, a useful technique is to place a light-toned subject against a darker background to increase the sense of depth – too bright a background will flatten the entire picture.

Background colours strongly influence the mood of a picture, dramatizing the image if the colour contrasts are vibrant, or suggesting tranquillity by colour harmonies. Remember that you can control the intensity of a background somewhat by using selective focus to soften colours. Outdoors, an eye-level viewpoint may give too busy a background. The low viewpoint adopted for the picture on the opposite page sets the subject against the sky. Alternatively, simplify the background by getting higher. Sometimes a strong colour area, such as a sunset sky, can itself become the starting point for a picture and prompt you to search for a suitable subject to set against the background.

A golden brown wall, occupying three-quarters of the picture area, gives this informal portrait strength without overwhelming the man.

The brilliant red inspired the picture below. Realizing its background potential, the photographer waited until a strong subject arrived – the sleek, black limousine.

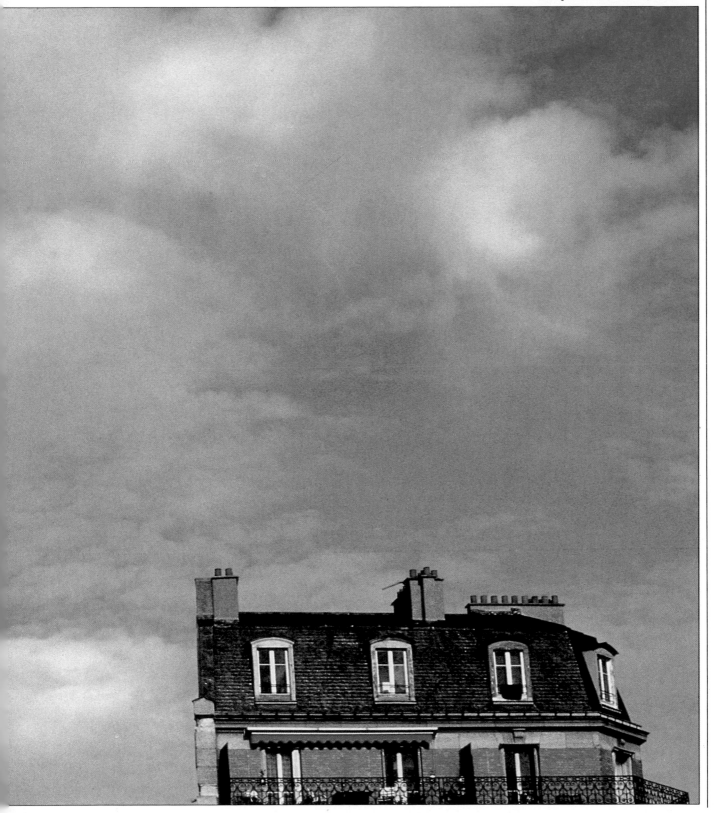

A cloudy blue sky can be striking enough to justify eliminating most of the foreground – the house merely balances the picture and provides a sense of scale.

THE COLOURS OF LIGHT

Colours are inseparable from the nature of the light that reveals them. Although midday sunlight and electronic flash combine the colour spectrum in such a way that their light appears white, most natural or artificial light sources are tinged with colour. Some forms of street lighting even look bright green. Objects illuminated by coloured light sources are subtly transformed – an effect that is more noticeable in photographs than to the eye. If you take pictures of people when the sun is low in the sky, skin tones become warmer, whereas by the light of fluorescent lamps, faces may appear a ghostly shade of green.

Other qualities of light also affect the colours of objects in photographs. The direction and intensity of light determine the contrast in the scene, for example. And strong, direct light usually makes colours lighter, while more general, softly diffused light may actually produce purer and richer hues. Thus, the time of day and the weather strongly influence the colours in your pictures. Understanding these effects and identifying the colour of a particular light source will help you to exploit the full colour potential of the scene you are photographing. Certain lighting conditions also raise special problems of exposure. As a guide, captions to some pictures in the section that follows specify the film and shutter speeds, and the aperture size, for a difficult situation.

Rio by twilight reveals the variety of colours emanating from the many different light sources. Ebbing sky light reflects as blue on the water, while the last direct rays of the setting sun turn patches of cloud pink or orange. The city's fluorescent street lights shine green, with dots of orange from an occasional tungsten lamp.

Direct sun

Sunny days have pleasant associations for most of us, and not surprisingly, people take more pictures in sunshine than in any other kind of light. To some extent, the brightness and intensity of direct sunlight simplify photography, and give you extra flexibility. You can use small apertures for great depth of field, or fast shutter speeds to freeze movement. Alternatively, you can load the camera with slow film to take advantage of fine grain and detail, as in the striking picture opposite. Colour accuracy is ensured because the light coming directly from a high sun is very close to white.

Making the most of the colours in the scene, however, may be unexpectedly difficult. Bright light can show colours in all their intensity – but only if the colours are perfectly exposed. The danger is that an area of bright colour – the red sail of a boat, for example – will be lighter than the surroundings, and will look washed out in the picture because you have exposed for the darker average tones. To overcome this, take the exposure reading from the colour area you want to look most brilliant, and if in doubt underexpose slightly – by a half stop or one stop. Sometimes, to show the strong colour at its best, you will have to accept underexposure elsewhere.

To prevent strong reflected light from washing out colours, use a polarizing filter. This will cut glare from shiny objects such as cars or other reflective surfaces such as water. The picture below shows how the same filter can also control over-intense light reflecting from the sky, giving you a strong blue in the upper part of the frame.

White sails drift gently on a placid blue lake, and the direct sun picks out each accent of white with brilliant clarity. To capture the full scene in finely etched detail, the photographer used a slow, fine-grain film (ISO 25).

In vivid red and yellow, a litter bin imposes a strong pattern of shapes and hues on a Florida beach scene. To darken the sky and make the bright colours of the hot plastic look deeper and richer, the photographer fitted a polarizing filter to the lens of his camera. When rotated to the correct orientation, such filters cut down glare and deepen the tone of areas of the sky that are away from the sun.

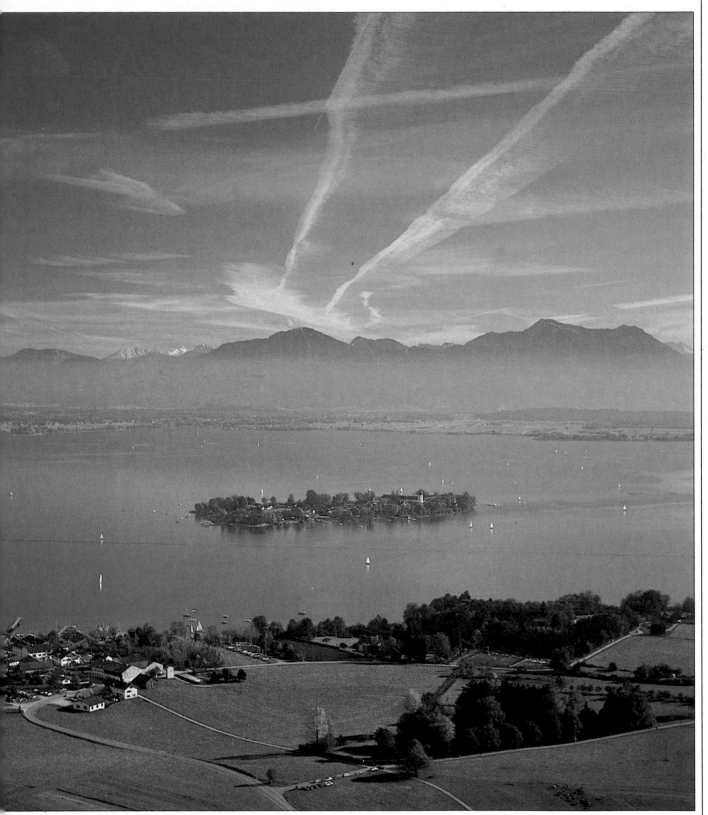

Low sun

Pictures lit by overhead sunlight conjure up impressions of hot, glittering afternoons, but the warm colours of low sun have more gentle connotations: morning light reminds us of the time just after dawn, when the sun's rays have yet to take the chill off the silent landscape. Sunset has a different, more romantic association – a lingering conclusion to a pleasant day.

Although our subjective impressions of morning and evening are quite different, these times of day are hard to tell apart on film. Low sun gives the same distinctive appearance to photographs taken early and late in the day. For a start, the raking light picks out textures and contours that are often masked when the sun is overhead. The long shadows are most obvious from above, so you can emphasize

them by choosing a high viewpoint – as the photographer has done for the picture of the beach chairs on the opposite page.

The other distinctive characteristic of low sunlight is its colour. The sun's rays on their oblique path through the atmosphere pass through more dust and water than they do at midday, and this scatters the shorter, bluer wavelengths. The redder, warmer colours that reach the earth give a rosy glow to pictures taken by their light.

We accept the redness of sunset and sunrise as natural, and often attractive, as in the picture here of the little girl by the poolside. But colour film tends to over-accentuate the effect, and you may sometimes prefer to reduce the red tinge with a filter from the bluish Kodak No. 82 series.

Splashing in the pool at *the end of a summer's day, this little girl is picked out in the warm colours of sunset. Far from needing correction, the reddish tones actually improve the picture. For a more formal portrait, or for subjects with a ruddy complexion, the warm cast might not be so flattering.*

Drying paint on an artist's palette forms a pattern of colour and texture when photographed from above. The photographer turned the board until the low sunlight fell obliquely across it, picking out the shining whorls of pigment.

Early morning light has emphasized the pattern and colours of beach seats (below). The photographer rose at dawn to take advantage of the long shadows, and to avoid the crowds that would have marred the perfect precision of the picture.

Backlight

The position of the sun always has a profound influence on the appearance of a photograph. But never so dramatically as when you point the camera directly toward the light source. This kind of lighting in a picture – usually called backlighting – works especially well with black-and-white film, because it produces highly graphic images that usually emphasize the outline and basic shape of subjects at the expense of surface texture, detail – and colour as well. Nevertheless, you can use the technique to take colour pictures of compelling simplicity.

If a subject is directly between the camera and the sun, the contrast range is likely to be so extreme that you will need either to overexpose the background or else to allow the shaded side of the subject – facing the lens – to become a dark silhouette. One exception is when the subject is transparent, allowing some light to pass through.

Because effective silhouette pictures in colour rely on the colour of the light source itself, morning and evening are the best time of day if you want to experiment. You may be able to use the warm, rich colours of sun and sky as the background. In the picture of the wooden pilings below, delicate pink light floods the whole picture as the water reflects the sky. To emphasize the subject's outline and retain the intensity of the background, take a meter reading directly from the sky, and perhaps increase the exposure indicated by one stop.

Although a silhouette is the normal effect of backlighting, the result is slightly different if the light source is just above or to one side of the subject. This produces a rim or halo around the subject, as in the picture of the girl below. You can make sure you retain the halo effect by taking a reading from the shadow area and then reducing exposure by two stops, and can experiment with the position and strength of the light to vary your effects.

Translucent subjects provide special opportunities for colourful backlit pictures. To capture the brilliant glow of the transmitted light, move in close and take a meter reading from the most important part of the subject – the petals of the yellow flowers, for example, in the picture opposite.

Outlined in sunlight, this window portrait would have been a silhouette but for the yellow light reflected from the girl's clothing. Look out for other similar reflecting surfaces to throw light into the shadows of a backlit picture.

Setting sun and high tide combine with mooring timbers in a spare, subtle image. By exposing for the background, the photographer reduced the seagull and its perch to their most basic and graphic outlines.

A vase of flowers glows with colour against the dark background of a walled city garden. By taking the picture against the light, the photographer used the delicate translucence of the tulip's petals to brighten the yellow.

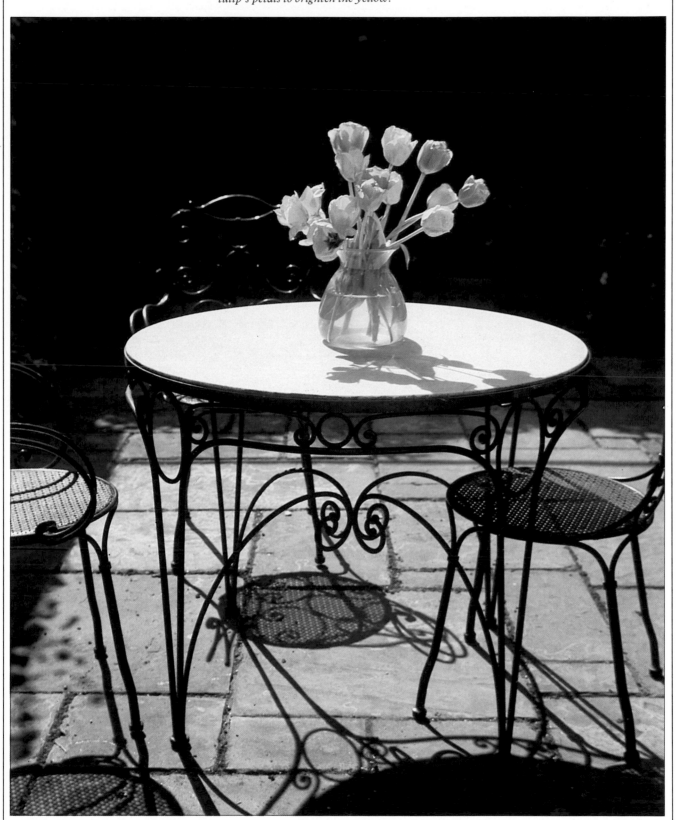

Diffused sunlight

You need to expose very carefully to bring out the brilliance of colours in direct sunlight, and to prevent them from becoming dissipated in glare and bouncing reflections. The pictures here show that colours often look richer in more diffused light. This is largely because contrast is reduced, making exposure easier to control. At the same time, the softer light helps to harmonize or balance colours – if that is your aim. And most important of all, diffused sunlight casts softer, less noticeable shadows. In portraiture, particularly, skin tones are thus recorded more accurately, and the whole image is less likely to be confused by the presence of deep, hard-edged shadows.

Light clouds and haze high in the sky diffuse light by redistributing the strongly directional rays of the sun across a larger part of the sky. The result is that shadows become less intense and their edges less sharp. Instead of being bright in the sun or dark in the shade, colours are brought closer together in tone. Provided the cloud cover is light, hues will retain their intensity. And, in the absence of hard shadows or reflected glare, the individual richness of the colours may actually increase. Because the key to showing any colour at full saturation is accurate exposure, the reduced contrast between naturally dark and light colours will allow you to choose an exposure that suits both. The varied greens of landscapes can thus be recorded with equal brilliance in the muted light. And in portraits, you can more easily blend and balance flesh tones, clothing and background colours.

A red fish, photographed in Kenya, glows with an almost unnatural brilliance against the equally vivid colours of the fisherman's shorts and T-shirt. The hazy sun reveals the full saturation of all the colours, without the intrusion of dark shadows. And the light keeps to a minimum the glare from the shiny scales.

Soft skin colours gave the key reading for this picture. But the sunlight, diffused by light clouds, restricted the range of tones. Thus reds and greens are correctly exposed also, and appear fully saturated. This light is ideal when you want to bring out the soft modelling of a face.

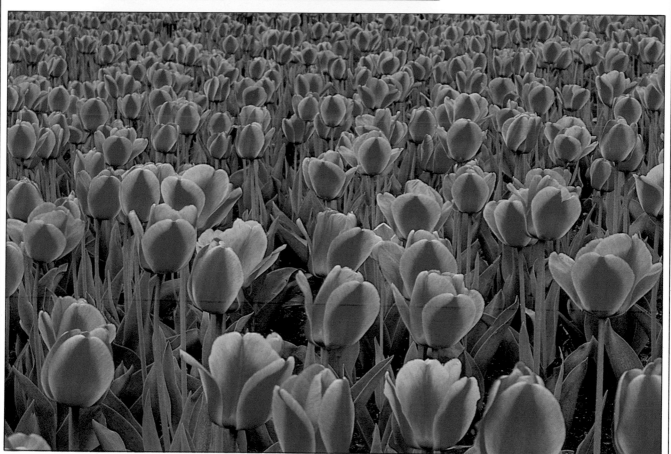

A sea of tulips vibrates with colour, every leaf, stalk and petal standing out in the soft light. Stronger sun might have made the flower heads gleam even more brightly, but the shadows created would have obscured the green parts of the plants, making them dark and underexposed on the film.

Haze, mist and fog

Photographs in dense haze, mist or fog produce some of the most delicate and subtle colour effects. These conditions not only weaken sunlight, but also spread the light around the subject, and themselves become part of the landscape. Haze is made up of microscopic particles suspended in the air — common during long, hot spells and also in polluted areas such as cities. The droplets of water that constitute mist and fog are larger and more often found at higher altitudes, or near rivers, lakes, or the sea.

Haze, mist and fog all thicken the atmosphere, acting as a kind of continuous filter. The result is that intense hues are muted to pastel. At the same time, colours tend to merge into a narrower range, creating images as beautiful and fragile as the harvesting scene below. In extremely dense mist or fog, the colours of a landscape may become almost monochromatic; hence the effects of these weather conditions can be useful if you want to give a soft overall tone to an image or to harmonize colours that would jar with each other in brighter, more direct light. And the absence of distracting detail can help you to appreciate the compositional qualities of a landscape more easily.

The softening of colour in haze, mist or fog becomes more pronounced with distance. The farther the subject is from the camera, the more simplified and delicate the image becomes, so that in a misty landscape, the different parts of the scene often appear to be arranged in receding layers of lighter and lighter colour, as in the picture of mountain ranges opposite. Sometimes, you can emphasize the sense of depth this produces by choosing a viewpoint that includes strong foreground colours.

Remember that the effect of fog and mist are not always regular and predictable. In a breeze, wisps of mist trail around trees, rocks and hillsides, often linking hues or emphasizing the colours of clear areas. And in dense but localized mist, of the kind that often hangs over wetlands early on a summer morning, trees and other subjects can appear almost in silhouette if the sun is directly behind them. Light itself then supplies the only colour, and in low sun, the scene may appear in delicate tones of orange or pink. You should look out for such unusual effects and exploit them by experimenting with viewpoint and camera angle. They open up marvellous opportunities for mood and atmosphere.

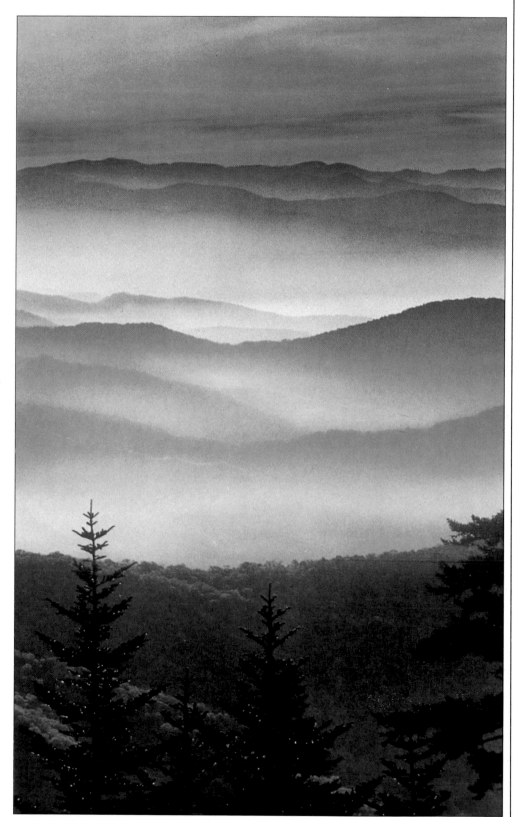

Late afternoon haze makes this Burmese agricultural scene almost monochromatic, turning everything a warm golden colour. The stubble of the field enhances the feeling of shimmering heat, and the pale rim of light around the group reveals a perfect choice of exposure.

Receding mountains are reduced here into broad washes of colour by early morning mist. This creates an imposing sense of depth as the planes of colour fade from green to lighter blues. The whole image is given an ethereal quality by the orange light tipping the farthest ridges as the sun penetrates the mist.

Rain and storm

Many photographers see bad weather as a sign to pack away the camera and go home. By doing so, you may miss opportunities for really exciting pictures. Dull, overcast lighting can certainly drain most of the colour from scenes and make everything seem drab. But often, light trapped beneath a lid of black rainclouds can give colours a dark, rich intensity never seen at other times. And although rain tends to soften and blur images, dampness often brings out subtle colours.

The spectacular brilliance of a thunderstorm, such as the one at far right, requires fast reactions – and, indeed, most storm-light effects are fleeting. The best chance of exploiting the vivid contrasts produced by a break in the clouds is to choose a high viewpoint. With a clear view over a wide area you can sometimes follow the bright trace of a shaft of sunlight moving across the landscape.

You do not have to wait until a storm is at its height to find dramatic light effects. A gathering storm can be equally impressive, especially in tropical climates, as the picture at bottom right shows. To preserve the relatively rich colours in the sunlight, and some sense of the impending darkness, be careful to avoid overexposure. You can emphasize the colour through contrast if you take a reading from the sunlit area, and then underexpose slightly to make the sky look still darker.

The picture below shows that the clouds which produce storm conditions may themselves form powerful aerial landscapes, especially if you photograph them from a distance with a wide-angle lens. The most exciting cloud formations of all are the tall, billowing thunderheads that form on hot afternoons in the tropics or in plains country such as the American Midwest.

The lowering blackness of the storm cloud gives this picture a power that seems all the more intense because the light is so muffled. The photographer waited until the cloud just covered the sinking sun, leaving shafts of light piercing through to gleam on the sea.

Raindrops on a rose change its colour to paler pink against a background muted both by the rain and by selective focusing. Delicate colour effects can often be achieved just after a rainstorm, provided the light is good.

Searing backlight from an electrical storm produced this remarkable night shot of a train stopped on a bridge. The photographer put the shutter on a "B" setting for a time exposure that has captured several lightning flashes.

Glowing light bathes a landscape in South-East Asia moments before a grey sky releases a deluge of monsoon rain. In this rare and beautiful light, the contrast between light foreground and dark background heightens the colour.

Dawn, dusk and night

Depending on climate, season and atmospheric conditions, the rising or setting sun can produce a remarkable range of flamboyant or subtle hues. At these times, the sky may be used as a richly coloured backdrop to a foreground city or landscape, or may provide sufficient pictorial interest to stand as a subject in its own right. Often, in order to bring out details of colours and cloud patterns in the sky, you will need to expose for the sky itself, leaving foreground elements to darken. With this in mind, try to choose objects in the foreground that will make strong silhouettes – or that have enough illumination of their own, as do the city buildings in the picture below right. A telephoto lens can emphasize the size and colour of a sinking or rising sun, or of the moon, when you want this to form the main subject, as in the photograph on the opposite page.

At dawn and dusk, it is not only the colours of sun and sky that vary from one moment to the next. The intensity of the light also changes rapidly. Therefore, keep rechecking your exposure reading every few minutes, and bracket exposures for safety. Because the light will be limited, if you are handholding the camera you will need a fast film, and a lens with a wide maximum aperture to allow a shutter speed fast enough to avoid the risk of camera shake. Often, time exposures are necessary, for which a tripod or other form of camera support is essential.

Cities at night are full of opportunities for colourful pictures – ranging from dramatic skylines to brilliant illuminated signs, multicoloured window displays, or the patterns of light made by moving traffic. Many of the most successful night pictures are in fact taken at dusk, when the sky retains some colour – and enough light for an exposure of perhaps 1/30 or 1/60 – yet street and domestic lights convey the impression of true night. In landscapes, the full moon itself can make an unusual light source for night-time colour shots. Contrary to popular belief, moonlight is white, not blue. Again, dusk is the best time for photographing the moon, because there will be enough light for a relatively short exposure. The moon moves more quickly than our eyes tell us, and if the exposure is longer than about a second, blur will begin to appear. In fact, the movement of the moon relative to the earth is such that it takes only about two minutes for the moon to cover the distance of its own diameter.

A neon sign, tightly framed, glows in luminous contrasting colours (above), emphasized by the use of daylight film. The exposure, with ISO 200 film was 1/60 at f/4.

Ablaze with colour, the radiant sunset sky creates a strangely surreal backdrop to the illuminated San Francisco skyline (ISO 400 film: 1/60 at f/5.6).

Pink light at dawn has tinted the distant mountain range, adding warmth to the cool blue of the sky and the snow. Dawn and dusk are marvellous times of day for shooting snow, seascapes, or any reflective subject that will pick up the colour of the light (ISO 200 film: 1/250 at f/8).

The full moon, through a 400 mm lens, stands out from the blue evening sky. At twilight, when it has just risen, the moon seems to loom largest in the sky. Enough light remains in the sky to show the hill and trees in silhouette (ISO 64 film: 1/60 at f/11).

Snow

Winter snowfalls create some of the most exceptional scenery, with marvellous opportunities for crisp colour contrast. But you need skill to preserve both the pure whiteness of snow and its sparkling, crystalline texture. Calculating the right exposure is crucial – snow tends to look grey if underexposed, and featureless if overexposed.

The camera's meter will usually read from the highlights in snow, and indicate an exposure that compensates for the intense brightness. Thus, the result of following the meter reading may be a less brilliant picture than you want. To avoid this, open one stop more than the metered reading. If taking several pictures, bracket the exposures to make sure of at least one good result. Perhaps the ideal is an exposure that records the brightest areas of snow as fractionally less than pure white – darkened just enough to show a hint of texture.

The sparkle and crisp texture of snow are revealed best by sunlight from the side or from slightly in front of the camera. Being highly reflective, snow tends to pick up any surrounding colours, and especially the colours of the sky. This can produce beautiful effects early or late in the day when the light is pink or golden. In overcast conditions, a yellowish No. 81C filter helps to compensate for the overall blue cast. But on a clear day, when snow appears white in direct sunlight and a strong blue in shaded areas, you cannot use a filter without altering the purity of the white at the same time. If you are photographing mountain scenery, use an ultraviolet (UV) filter to cut down the overall blue cast caused by the scattered ultraviolet light at high altitudes. In order to enhance the deep blue of the sky, contrasting with the crisp white of the snow, you can use a polarizing filter.

Two skiers in packed snow provide warm colour against the coolness of white and blue. Using ISO 64 film, the meter reading was 1/500 at f/11, but the picture was taken at f/8 to retain the whiteness.

The golden light of a low sun early in the day bathes the snow with the warmth of the reflected colour. Notice how the slanting light glints on ice melting as the temperature rises.

Shaded foreground snow, still reflecting blue light from the upper sky, blends softly with sky tinged by the setting sun nearer the horizon. Snow allows you to make handheld exposures at dusk even when little light remains in the sky.

A latticework of snow in a fence (below) creates a pattern by breaking up the bright colours of playing children. Winter landscapes are full of such opportunities.

Tungsten lighting/I

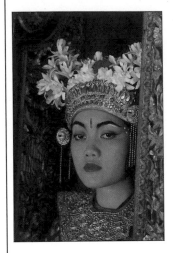

A Balinese girl looks out from a setting of carved splendour. Tungsten lighting used with tungsten-type film gives the scene a golden glow; daylight film would have made the tones warmer (ISO 160 film: 1/30 at f/2.8).

While most photographs are taken in daylight, opportunities for colour photographs of equal beauty and interest emerge when artificial light provides the main illumination. The most common form of artificial light for photography is flash, which has approximately the colour characteristics of daylight. Often, however, room or street lights provide sufficient illumination for a long exposure with a tripod – or they may appear in the picture as an inherent part of the subject. These lights usually have tungsten filaments, with a warmer colour than daylight, showing as orange on daylight film.

For convincing natural results, you may want to correct the orange cast back to normal by using the techniques described on pages 24-25. On the other hand, you may use the orange successfully to inject more colour into your pictures. As a general light source, tungsten provides an overall warm glow that is often attractive. In the same way, individual tungsten lights in a picture taken in very low light or darkness will show as points of orange or yellow light, enlivening the scene. Think about such colour effects before deciding that you need to use a conversion filter or a tungsten-balanced film.

Varied wooden surfaces create a rich interplay of tone and texture – the daylight film used records a delicate orange cast from tungsten room lights, producing an inviting feeling (ISO 64 daylight film: 1/2 at f/5.6).

Large cities are usually full of tungsten lighting at night, and even more so on festive occasions. The photograph on the left shows the Place de la Madeleine in Geneva, with a merry-go-round the centre of attraction. The overall feeling of warmth in the colours is characteristic of tungsten light recorded on daylight film (ISO 64 film: 1/8 at f/4).

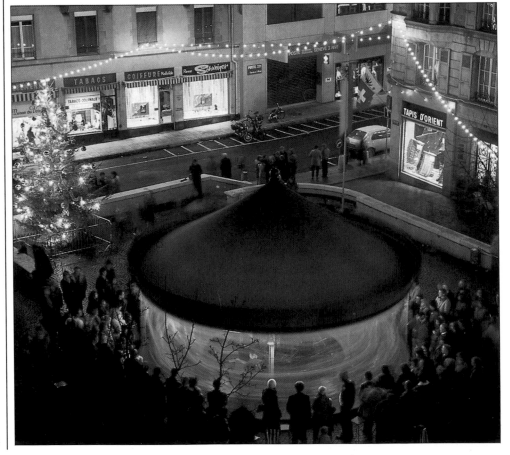

A highway at night gives opportunities to photograph spectacular tungsten light effects. At right, two main sources create contrasting patterns, the regular lines of the lights acting as a foil to the curving trails left by car tail lights during a long exposure (ISO 64 film: 1 sec. at f/5.6).

Tungsten lighting/2

Mixed lighting is characteristic of many night-time photographs, particularly at dusk, when ebbing daylight may provide as much or more light than tungsten or other lights that have been switched on. While sometimes presenting tricky problems in terms of exposure or film choice, this kind of lighting also produces some of the most attractive colour effects. This is particularly true when one source of light predominates in the picture while another provides contrasting colour accents.

The basic rule for mixing tungsten and daylight is to decide which light source dominates, and choose a film balanced to that. Outdoors, just before nightfall, the main illumination comes usually from the daylight. On daylight film, the tungsten lights will appear orange, as in the pictures below. When there is less daylight than tungsten light, you could decide to use a conversion filter – or a slide film balanced for tungsten light – in order to show tungsten-lit colours more accurately.

The choice between daylight and tungsten light

film becomes more crucial for pictures of interiors in which you need to use a mixture of daylight and room lighting. If daylight from windows predominates, and particularly if the windows appear in the picture, there is no need to change from daylight film. The warm orange of tungsten room lights will add to the atmosphere, as in the interior scene on the opposite page.

In the early evening, or if the windows are small, the situation may be different, with the main light coming from the room lamps. To avoid everything turning orange, you should use a tungsten-light slide film – or a No. 80A blue conversion filter. Light from the windows will appear in the resulting picture as a shade of blue.

If you are undecided about whether daylight or tungsten dominates, always opt for daylight film. The warm glow of tungsten light exposed on this film is usually more acceptable than the cold blue of daylit subjects recorded on tungsten film, and looks closer to normal experience.

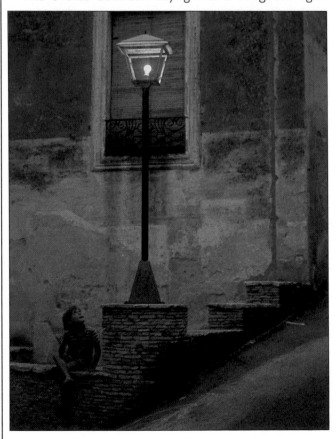

A streetlight glows in gathering dusk – daylight film records most of the scene in its true colors, but tints the lamp a warm orange (ISO 200 film: 1/30 at f/2).

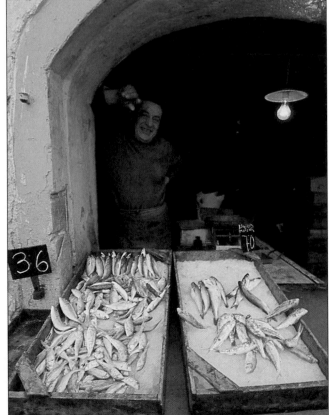

The fish stall is lit by daylight, but the fish seller is lit by tungsten. On daylight film, his face looks orange (ISO 64 film: 1/60 at f/5.6).

A **hotel lobby** *in Monte Carlo is lit by tungsten lamps, but daylight floods in through the glass doors. On daylight film, the tungsten-lit ceiling looks a rich orange, suiting the opulent decor. With tungsten light film or a colour filter, the ceiling would have appeared in true colours, but the entrance would have looked a chilly blue. The photographer rightly chose to use daylight film unfiltered (ISO 200 film: 1/125 at f/4).*

A **Palm Springs street** *is lit bright by tungsten shop lights of varying strengths. Here, the use of tungsten film adds interest by deepening the dusk sky (ISO 25 film: 2 secs at f/5.6)*

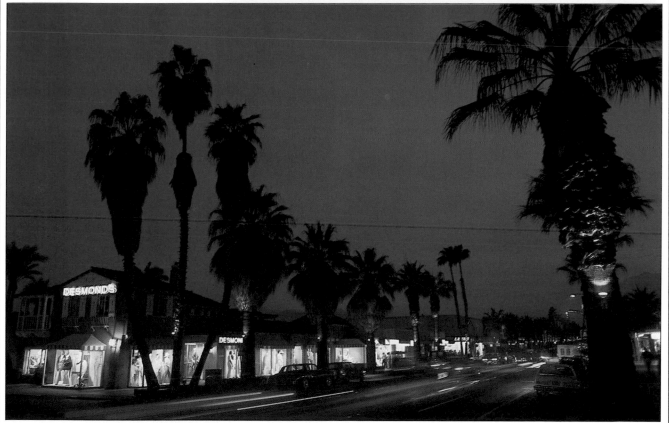

Other artificial lighting/1

A tungsten lamp produces light by heating a thin coil of wire inside a glass bulb, but some other common light sources do not rely on heat. Fluorescent lights and other vapour lights such as sodium and mercury work instead by passing an electrical current through a gas- or vapour-filled tube. Light produced by the resulting spark nearly always has a distinctive colour – for example, sodium lighting, which is widely used on roads and industrial premises, is yellow. Sometimes the colour of vapour lights gives visual interest to scenes that might otherwise look mundane. But when you are using vapour lighting to illuminate other subjects – especially people – the colour cast may simply look wrong.

Sodium and mercury vapour lighting produces effects on daylight film similar to those produced by tungsten lights, but the colour casts cannot be eliminated in the same way. Whereas the light wavelengths of tungsten lamps range across the whole spectrum – but with a bias towards red – vapour lamps other than fluorescent tubes produce light of just one or two colours. Putting a filter over a camera lens can only remove colours, not add them. Thus, although you can filter out the excess of red light from tungsten, you cannot put back the wavelengths missing from sodium or mercury light, whatever film or filter you use. The best thing to do is to accept the situation and make a virtue of the resulting colour. For example, all the pictures here were taken on daylight film. In portraiture, where usually natural skin tones are important, you can introduce another light source, such as electronic flash, to light the foreground and counteract the colour cast in the main area of the picture.

Fluorescent strip lamps differ from other vapour lamps, because their glass tubes carry a coating of phosphors, which make the tube glow with light in a broad range of wavelengths. Although this produces a light that looks white, all but the most expensive lamps are deficient in red or magenta, and pictures taken by their light have a greenish tint. The actual shade of green depends on the type of tube and its age. If you are taking a picture in fluorescent light, and colour accuracy is important, you may need to make a series of exposures with different colour compensation filters. But generally, a CC 30M (magenta) filter, or a special "fluorescent to daylight" filter will help.

City streetlights usually are either sodium or mercury vapour lamps. In the picture above, the photographer used a long exposure with the camera on a tripod and took advantage of the striking colour of mercury lamps to turn roadside snow into a turquoise background for the lights of the passing cars *(ISO 200 film: 4secs at f/11).*

A pool enclosure, lit by fluorescent tubes, seems to be suffused with green light. The colour is seen most clearly where the lights shine directly onto the blue-grey wall. The effect produced is one of subterranean chill and eeriness *(ISO 100 film: 1/60 at f/5.6).*

The Jefferson Memorial
(above) appears the yellow
colour of its floodlights. To the
eye, the building would have
appeared much whiter, but
complete colour correction is
not necessary to achieve an
effective picture (ISO 400
film: 1/30 at f/2).

A statue in Brasilia glows
an unearthly green in the
light of mercury floodlights.
Such monuments often look
at their best by night, when
the strange and upredictable
colours of their lights show
up strongly in photographs
(ISO 200 film: 1/8 at f/5.6).

Other artificial lighting/2

In most twilight or night views of cities, every type of light vies for attention, producing a variety of lurid colours on film. Confronted with such colour bonanzas, there is little point in attempting to balance the film to the light. Daylight film without filters will show greens, yellows or blues from vapour lamps, red or orange from tungsten, and the pulsing colours of neon lights – all mingled with whatever varied hues the last rays of the sun create in the atmosphere. The effects can be spectacular, and the shot on the right shows just the kind of drama a mixture of colours can create.

Occasionally you will be able to exploit these possibilities in a more controlled way. If you remember that vapour light is likely to produce a strong colour cast on daylight film, you can contrast illuminated objects with the entirely different colours of the sky behind – as in the picture of a parked car below, which would have looked much less remarkable in ordinary lighting conditions.

Multiple light sources illuminate this industrial complex. In addition to the setting sun, mercury and sodium vapour lamps shine on buildings and roads. Offices glow with fluorescent light, and tungsten lights from passing cars streak through the picture. Wisely abandoning attempts at colour correction, the photographer took full advantage of the contrasts.

A beach-side parking lot shines with the luminous green of fluorescent strip-lighting. Against the deep pink of the twilight sky, car and blank concrete take on an eerie starkness. Although the artificial light looked white to the eye, the photographer anticipated the more striking colour that film would show.

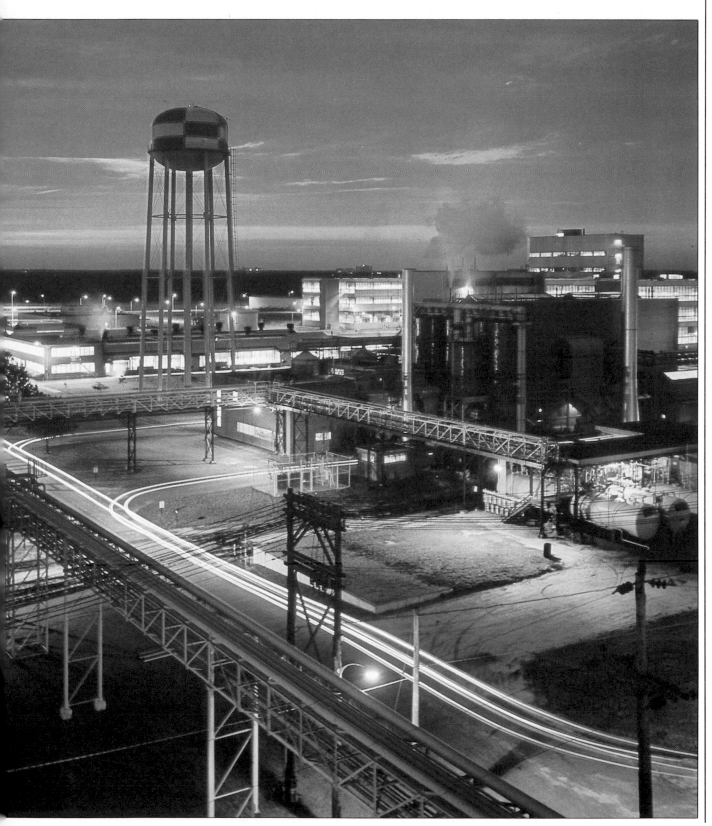

Flames

The light of flames from burning candles or oil lamps, matches or fires provides the most natural form of illumination other than daylight. Although light is unpredictable, flames create such atmospheric images that pictures lit by this source can be enormously rewarding. Most flames burn at far lower temperatures than do indoor lights and so produce light of a distinctly orange, even red, colour. Photographed on tungsten-balanced film, flame-lit scenes look a natural pale orange and on daylight film, which was used for all the pictures on these two pages, the warmer orange cast still looks acceptable, because even our eyes generally perceive flames as red or orange.

If you are taking pictures of only the flames themselves, accurate exposure is not particularly important – overexposed flames still appear yellowish while underexposure simply intensifies the red. Such moving flames as sparks or fireworks look attractive both when frozen by a fast shutter speed or when allowed to trace streaks of light during a time exposure. Choosing an exposure to record both the bright flames and the subjects they dimly illuminate is more of a problem. Place the subject as near as possible to the flame to minimize the brightness range. And read exposure from the subject, allowing the flames to be overexposed if necessary. You are likely to need fairly slow shutter speeds, even with high-speed ISO 400 film, and because exposure will be difficult to measure accurately, bracket your shots. Do not be tempted to supplement the light – using flash to photograph people around a campfire, for example, can destroy the entire mood of the scene.

A blacksmith, his face glowing red in the light from the fire, forges a horseshoe. Daylight supplements the flames, providing the general illumination for the smithy (ISO 400 film: 1/30 at f/4).

A row of houses, lit by a giant festival bonfire across the street, seems to be on fire as the flames reflect in the windows – an effect enhanced by the red light (ISO 200 film: 1/15 at f/2).

A glass of brandy, being warmed in a candle flame, makes an appealing still-life. The orange light creates mood, but is barely strong enough for an effective exposure (ISO 400 film: 1/30 at f/2).

A wood fire burns with orange flames in the snow. The scene is lit entirely by daylight, giving a very slight blue tint because of the overcast sky. The winter's day, stark trees and black dress make a monochromatic, even colourless, image, brought to life by the glow of the fire (ISO 100 film: 1/125 at f/8).

Fireworks burst orange and white over New York harbour, contrasting with the fluorescent green of the floodlit Statue of Liberty behind. Among burning light sources, fireworks are uniquely varied in colour (ISO 400 film: 1/30 at f/8).

USING COLOUR CREATIVELY

Most photography records the appearance of life, more or less unaltered by the imagination of the person who took the picture. In colour photography, basic techniques such as exposing correctly or matching the right film to the light source are used toward this end. But having understood that colour is attractive for its own sake, or has the power to move us, you may want to steer farther away from the literal representation of things. Often, by breaking the rules you can change the image that appears in the viewfinder and make a picture that will surprise the viewer – and perhaps yourself as well.

 Some of the pictures on the following 16 pages show colours that are blurred, streaked by movement, or so isolated from their context by a close-range camera position that they make no literal sense. In others, reflections show subjects distorted beyond recognition. And in still others, filters have fragmented the colours of a scene, or introduced new and unearthly hues. Used skilfully, unorthodox techniques can allow you an artist's freedom to produce images of original beauty – patterns in which the colours do not define objects but serve your own creative purpose.

Condensation running down a window turns the image of the sun to the glittering texture of iced orange. Such a picture has no easily recognizable subject – our simple enjoyment of the colour is more than enough.

Colour and movement/I

Vigorous colours can add zing to action pictures frozen by fast shutter speeds – for example a ski racer in red angled against a wall of blue ice. Less obviously, perhaps, movement recorded with a slow shutter can produce colour effects of a unique and subtle kind. Colours blurred or streaked across the film have a lightness and fluidity all their own. And you can use movement to separate colours altogether from subject matter, and form abstract patterns of lines and swirls.

Some of the fun of streaking colour in a photograph lies in the uncertainty of the final image: you have to take some chances with this technique. However, you can exercise choice over the colours of subject and background, the speed and rhythm of movement, and the length of exposure – all of which have a bearing on the result. For the most dramatic results, choose a light coloured or illuminated subject with a dark background. The faster the subject is moving – and the slower the shutter speed – the more the colours will be diffused and streaked. Alternatively, you may be able to find a strong, static colour in the background and contrast this with a moving subject that is softly blurred.

Lines surging upward in a modern building (right) seem to pass through a descending figure. Having spotted the composition, the photographer set a slow shutter speed and waited for someone to arrive. The solid bars of colour in the background emphasize the muted hues and blurred shape of the dematerialized figure.

Deckchair canvases billowing in the breeze stream with fluid colours (above). The photographer used a wide aperture to obtain a shallow depth of field, so that only the middle chair is in focus.

A fairground in full swing throws out disembodied loops of coloured light against a deep night sky (below). The picture's drama comes from the brilliance and whirling motion of the subject, combined with the still, dark background.

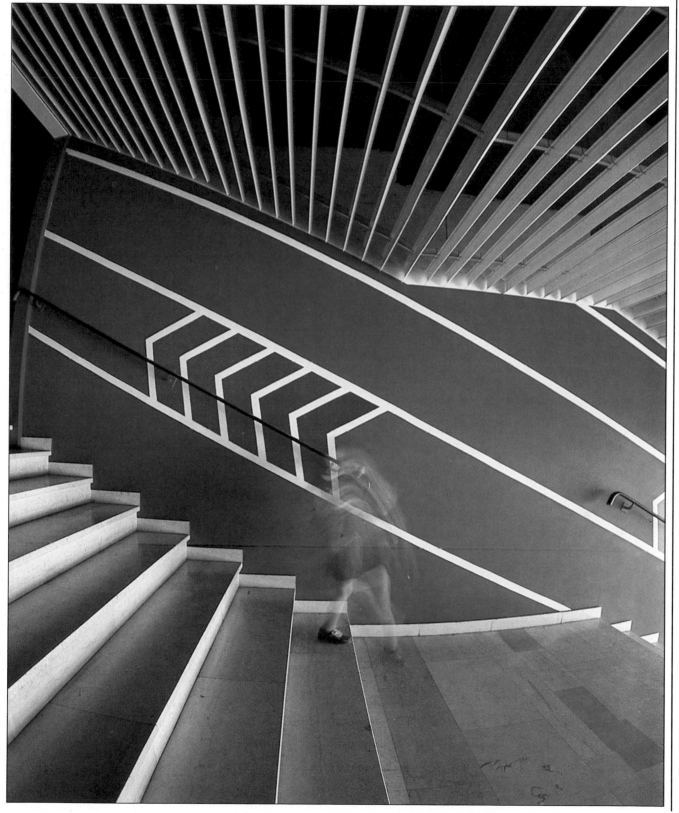

Colour and movement/2

In addition to blurring moving subjects with a slow shutter speed, you can introduce streaks of light and colour into your picture by deliberately not keeping the camera steady. A long exposure will still be needed – perhaps 1/4 to a full second. Simply loosen your grip and move, shake or jar the camera during the exposure. Different movements will give smooth streaks, abrupt angles or graceful swirls. However, anticipating the final results can be difficult and you must be prepared to experiment.

Deliberate movement of the camera can be used with both static and moving subjects. If your subject is passing across the frame, you will need to pan the camera to follow the movement. At the same time, try giving a slight jerk or even twist of the camera. With luck, the subject will retain a recognizable shape but be surrounded by liquid colour, as in the picture of a jumping horse below.

An alternative way of breaking up the colours in a picture is to use a zoom lens and operate the zoom control during an exposure of about 1/4. The resulting effect of streaks radiating from the centre of the image can give a vivid impression of movement, even when the subject is stationary.

The lights of Hong Kong skyscrapers (above) shoot into darkness like exploding fireworks. From a height, the photographer focused on the buildings across the street, then changed the zoom setting of the lens during exposure.

A horse and rider clear a jump against a backdrop of swirling colour. Apart from following the movement of the horse with a panning technique, the photographer shook the camera to add fluid waves to the streaking.

White water bursts toward the camera as a kayak makes a difficult turn. Rather than using a fast shutter speed to freeze the movement, the photographer moved the zoom control during the exposure to increase the sense of energy.

Abstract colour/1

You can give your pictures a striking abstract quality quite easily by exploiting bold colour areas. All you need to do is to frame the subject so that colours rather than recognizable forms are emphasized.

A good way of making colour abstract is to exclude part of the subject. We identify things largely by their outlines and the context in which we find them. Isolated by tight or unconventional framing, objects appear as a two-dimensional arrangement in the picture. The effect of the yellow dress opposite was achieved in this way. By cropping out the girl's head with the frame, the photographer has removed the obvious centre of attention and concentrated on the composition as an arrangement of colours. Alternatively, you can tilt the camera so that the subject, seen from an unusual angle, becomes less important than the colours. You can even try taking the picture with the subject deliberately out of focus to make the shapes less distinct and more to be enjoyed as areas of colour.

Lighting is an important factor in emphasizing colour at the expense of literal representation. Flat light on an overcast day can be used to give a two-dimensional effect because there are no shadows to throw objects into relief. On the other hand, direct sunlight, provided there is no glare, can illuminate colours and bring out strong contrasts between them, producing strikingly vivid effects.

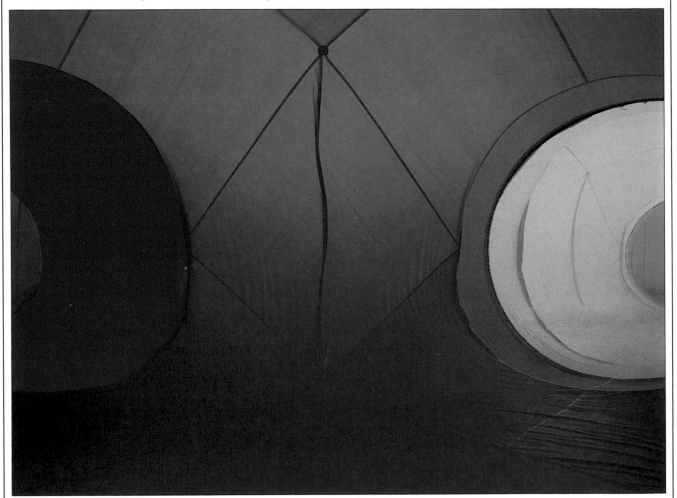

An inflatable play space provides the setting for a boldly abstract composition. The photographer framed the scene to balance the three strong colours of the translucent material and has excluded any details that could act as reference points to help interpret the subject.

Abstract colour/2

Colour patterns, formed by natural and manufactured objects alike, make fascinating subjects for abstract photographs. As with any abstract image, the key to a successful composition lies in framing to eliminate unwanted details.

Anything assembled in a series – panels in a fence, bridge girders, or a row of soldiers – forms a pattern, and tends to flatten the picture. Subjects containing strong lines and only a few bold colours make the most effective images. With an open pattern, as in the photograph of children's swingboats opposite, the background can become part of the design.

A diagonal viewpoint often strengthens the sense of pattern – particularly if you use a telephoto lens. By giving an impression of foreshortening to the image, telephoto lenses produce pictures with a two-dimensional character – ideal when you want to emphasize patterns of colour – as the picture below of a military band demonstrates.

A military band makes a dense colour pattern dominated by the red and black of the soldiers' uniforms. From this distance, the ranks of guardsmen appear closer together than they really are – an effect that the photographer managed by using a 300mm telephoto lens to fill the frame with pattern.

Playground swings impose an intricate lattice framework on the merging hues of sand, sea and sky behind. Having moved around the subject in order to find the most effective composition, the photographer closed in from a diagonal viewpoint.

Finding colour in reflections

Reflections – found in all kinds of settings, indoors and outdoors – offer the photographer particularly unusual colour effects. Even a mirror gives back a subtly changed image of a coloured object, and less faithful reflective surfaces can make colours appear to flow, swirl or bend. Just a slight unevenness in a shiny surface – such as ripples on water – will alter and distort a reflection. The patina of time-worn brass, gold or tarnished silver will overlay a reflected image with added colour and texture. Chrome, a highly reflective surface, produces clear, bright images, but unusual effects are still possible because the curved chromework on cars and motor-cycles strongly distorts anything reflected.

Because colours are usually muted when reflected, you will get the most vivid effects in bright lighting. If morning or afternoon sun illuminates buildings on one side of a river, leaving the water in shade, reflections viewed from the opposite bank are far more intense than they are on a cloudy day, when the entire scene is uniformly lit. However, sometimes an effect depends on soft, diffuse lighting – as in the picture below, in which an expanse of still water echoes the soft colours of the scene.

To photograph reflections on a small surface, for which a close camera position is necessary, you can use a wide-angle lens or a small aperture to get sharpness in depth. Alternatively, focus only on the surface: the reflection will then appear as a blurred wash of colour. It might seem that the reflecting surface and the reflected image would always be equally in or out of focus, but for focusing purposes the image is farther away – light has to travel from the subject to reach the reflecting surface.

A lake mirrors the delicate hues of a pastoral landscape at sunrise (left). The glass-like surface of the water gives a reflection with only slight distortion, so that the effect is of a twin image.

A city street, slick after rain, reflects lights as a haze of colours (below left). By focusing on the surface of the road near the camera, the photographer has added to the soft, blurred effect.

A brass plaque in London adds its own mellow tones to the red reflection of a passing bus (below). The photographer focused on the plaque and waited for the bus to appear in view.

A small puddle beside
a cobbled street reflects
part of a sunlit building.
Strong lighting and a well-
judged angle give clarity
and definition to the image.

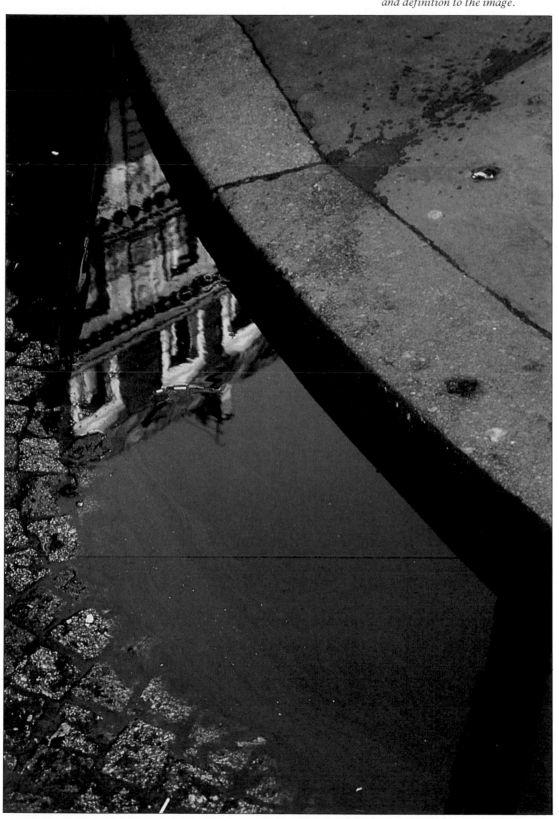

Colour in close-up

Moving in extremely close can exclude distracting details and emphasize the strong colours to be found in relatively small parts of many subjects. You can even fill the picture area with patches of colour so tiny that they would normally go unnoticed. To move in very close you need special accessories, such as inexpensive supplementary lenses, a macro lens or a set of extension tubes. These allow you to achieve tight, graphic compositions in which the colours almost seem to leap out of the picture.

Manufactured items often contain strong dyes that are particularly vivid in isolated close-up. The little pencil sharpener below is an example of the way that, with careful composition, an ordinary object can take on a significance and interest that would never be evident to the eye. In nature, too, colourful subjects can benefit from close-up treatment. Few flower heads are big enough to fill the frame at a normal distance. But by moving in to concentrate on details rather than recording the overall appearance, you can isolate the vibrant relationship between colours or give emphasis to a rich single colour. The purple flower below would never have looked so pure and bright in colour had its full shape been included in the picture. The strongly three-dimensional shape of flowers can be difficult to keep in focus because of the limited depth of field in close-up photography. This is not a disadvantage when your aim is to exploit only one colour rather than to achieve the sharp clarity of botanical illustration. However, if you are photographing the intricate, multiple colour patterns of plants or insects, when the sharp edges of the colour areas are vital to the effect, you need to use an aperture small enough for the whole subject to be in focus.

A characteristic that is worth seeking out in nature is iridescence. The wings or carapaces of certain insects shine with a rainbow-like spectrum, which changes as the insect moves. Iridescence is also found in the feathers of some birds, perhaps most spectacularly in the peacock's, as shown in the photograph on the opposite page.

A butterfly wing (above) is seen as an intricate texture of scales when photographed at life size with a 50mm macro lens. Such close-ups of nature can reveal bold, even extraordinary, colour patterns and markings.

The vibrant petals of a flower fill the frame with richly saturated colour (above). Including only the centre of the bloom has restricted the colour range for a concentrated effect, achieved with a macro lens.

A red pencil sharpener contrasts startlingly with a green background (left). By closing in with an extension tube, the photographer made a strongly graphic picture from a small, everyday household object.

A peacock feather (right) shimmers with iridescence in a picture taken by fitting a supplementary close-up lens over a normal 50mm lens. The area of dark blue was carefully included to set off the shining lighter greens.

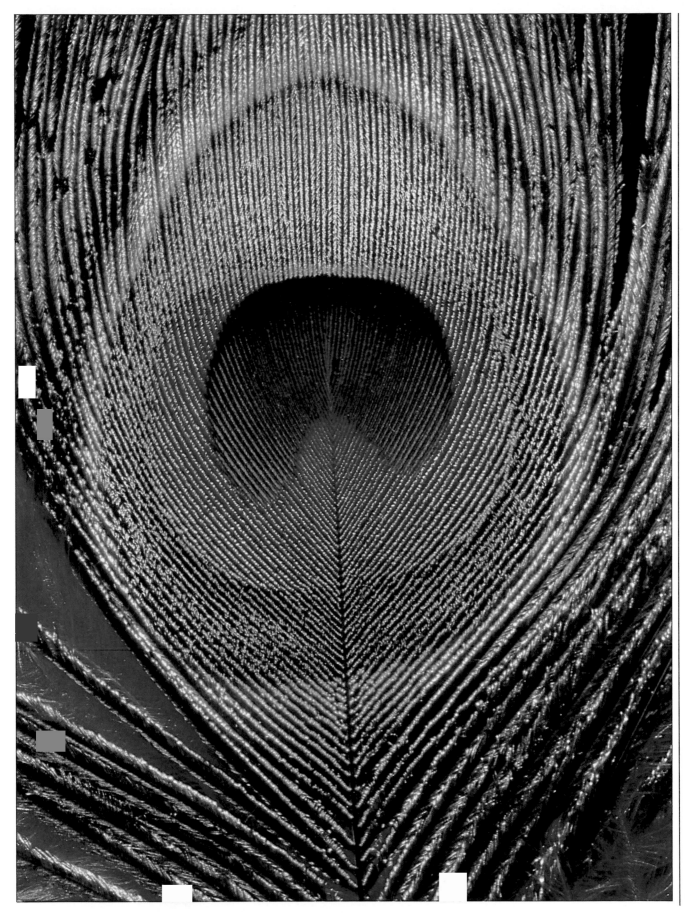

Special filters for colour/1

The most direct way of manipulating the colours of a photograph is to use a filter over the lens. Most filters are designed to make technical adjustments – for example, to match the light to the colour balance of the film in the camera. But many filters are now available that have a different purpose: to create dramatic images by altering the existing colours or by revealing hues that were hardly evident before.

The most basic filters of this type simply give the image an overall colour tinge. Pale-coloured filters have a subtle effect, modulating the colours in the scene and perhaps exaggerating a dominant hue. More strongly coloured filters can influence every part of the image, creating entirely new and even unrealistic colours. The shadow of the tree below has been bathed in lurid and mysterious colour by a deep green filter, making the picture look like a night shot even though it was taken in daylight.

Some coloured filters have only half their glass or plastic tinted, with a smooth transition from the colour to a clear part. Known as graduated filters or half filters, these can be rotated, allowing you to colour whichever section of the image you choose. Alternatively, you can try using two graduated filters to colour different parts of the image, as in the example at right, in which the horizon separates the picture into two areas of heightened colour to produce a dreamlike effect.

A tree's shadow falling on a rough stone wall made a strong and interesting image but one that lacked colour, so the photographer used a deep green filter. Daylight seems transformed into a strange artificial glow, with the green suffusing every part of the powerful image.

Special filters for colour/2

Some filters that have no colour in themselves can have dramatic effects on the way colours appear in photographs. Instead of modifying the colour of the light passing into the camera, they cause a controlled deterioration of the image. For example, diffusion or soft-focus filters use various kinds of mat surfaces to dull a picture's sharpness very slightly, so that details are obscured and the colours merge softly into each other. Mist and fog filters change the image in a comparable way, but they have a much stronger effect. As their name suggests, they introduce a misty appearance, spreading out the colour of the bright parts of the picture. With an appropriate subject, this hazy look can add a nostalgic or romantic feeling to your photographs – as in the picture of the girl in a landscape below.

Starburst and diffraction filters conjure up quite another mood – one of vibrancy and excitement. They are etched with varying patterns of grooves that can have different effects. A starburst filter creates a brilliant star from each bright point of light in the image. The number of points in each star depends on the filter. For example, in the picture of the neon sign at top right, the photographer used a two-point starburst filter. Diffraction filters go one step further: with surfaces covered by a complex grid of minute grooves, they split the rays of the star into a rainbow-like spectrum.

A girl in a landscape seems surrounded by a soft, hazy, almost dreamlike atmosphere, created by a mist filter that also spreads and emphasizes the pink of her dress.

Neon dancers gain extra sparkle from the grooves on a starburst filter (left), which caused the coloured lights in the picture to streak across the image as brightly ghosted lines.

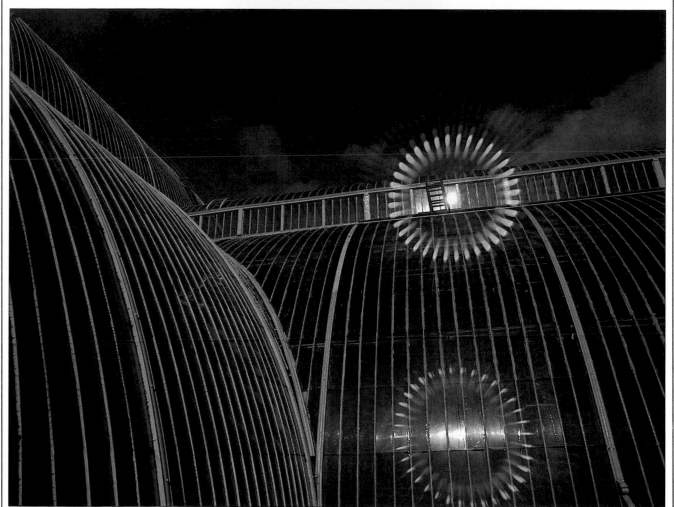

A huge greenhouse gleams in the sun. The photographer used a diffraction filter to create coloured haloes around the points of light caused by the sun's reflection.

Glossary

Aperture
The opening in a lens that admits light. Except in very simple cameras, the aperture can be varied in size to regulate the amount of light passing through the lens to the film.

Backlighting
A form of lighting where the principal light source shines toward the camera, and lights the subject from behind.

Bracketing
A way to ensure accurate exposure by taking several pictures of the same subject at slightly different exposure settings above and below (that is, bracketing) the presumed correct setting.

Cast
An overall tinge of a particular colour in a print or transparency. Colour casts often occur when the light source illuminating the subject of a photograph is not matched to the film.

Colour negative (print) film
Film processed as a negative image from which positive prints can be made.

Colour transparency (slide) film
Film giving direct colour positives in the form of transparencies. It is also known as reversal film.

Colour temperature
Term describing the colour quality (particularly the redness or blueness) of the light source.

Complementary colours
Two contrasting colours that produce an achromatic shade, white, grey or black, when mixed. Complementary colour pairs are important in colour films and printing processes. Traditionally, the pairs used are red-cyan, green-magenta and blue-yellow.

Daylight film
Film balanced to give accurate colours when exposed to a subject lit by daylight or light of similar colour-temperature – for example, electronic flash.

Depth of field
The zone of acceptable sharp focus in a picture, extending in front of and behind the plane of the subject that is most precisely focused by the lens.

Exposure
The total amount of light allowed to pass through a lens to the film, as controlled by both aperture size and shutter speed. The exposure selected must be tailored to the film's sensitivity to light, indicated by the film speed rating. Hence overexposure means that too much light has created a slide or print that is too pale. Conversely, underexposure means that too little light has resulted in a dark image.

Film speed
A film's sensitivity to light, rated numerically so that it can be matched to the camera's exposure controls. The two most commonly used scales, ASA (American Standards Association) and DIN (Deutsche Industrie Norm), are now superseded by a new system known as ISO (International Standards Organization), which amalgamates the ASA and DIN ratings.

Filter
A glass, plastic or gelatin screen placed in front of the lens to alter the appearance of an image. Colour filters work by absorbing selected wavelengths of light.

Flash
A very brief but intense burst of artificial light, used in photography as a supplement or alternative to any existing light in a scene.

Fluorescent light see VAPOUR LAMP

Focal length
The distance, usually given in millimetres, between the optical centre of a lens and the point at which rays of light from objects at infinity are brought to focus. In general, the greater the focal length of a lens, the smaller and more magnified the part of the scene it includes in the picture frame.

Graduated filter
A filter in which a clear and coloured half gradually blend into each other. Such a filter can be used, for example, to enliven a dull sky in a landscape without affecting the rest of the image.

Grain
The granular texture appearing to some degree in all processed photographic materials. In black-and-white photographs the grains are minute particles of black metallic silver that constitute the dark areas of a photograph. In colour photographs the silver is removed chemically, but tiny blotches of dye retain the appearance of the grain. The more sensitive – or fast – the film, the coarser the grain will be.

Latitude
The ability of a film to record an image satisfactorily if exposure is not exactly correct. Black-and-white and colour print films generally have more latitude than colour transparency films.

Polarizing filter
A filter that changes the vibration pattern of the light passing through it, used chiefly to remove unwanted reflections from a photographic image or to darken the blue of the sky.

Primary colours
Blue, green and red – the colours of light that mixed together equally make white light, and, when mixed in various combinations, can make any other colour. Saturated colours are "pure" colours that reflect only one or two primaries – when a third primary is introduced the colour is "de-saturated" toward white, grey or black.

Saturated colour see PRIMARY COLOUR

Shutter
The camera mechanism that controls the duration of the exposure.

Stop
A comparative measure of exposure. Each standard change of the shutter speed or aperture (for example, from 1/60 to 1/125 or from f/2.8 to f/4) represents a stop, and doubles or halves the light reaching the film. On some cameras you can make settings in between the standard marks – usually in half-stops.

Tripod
A three-legged camera support. The legs (usually collapsible) are hinged together at one end to a head to which the camera is attached.

Tungsten light
A very common type of electric light for both domestic and photographic purposes – named after the filament of the metal tungsten through which the current passes. Tungsten light is much warmer (more orange) than daylight or electronic flash, and you must use a filter with daylight-balanced colour film to compensate for this and reproduce colours accurately. Alternatively, use tungsten-balanced slide film.

Ultraviolet
A form of electromagnetic radiation close in wavelength to light. UV radiation is invisible to the human eye, but can affect film, sometimes causing a blue cast unless removed by a filter.

Vapour lamp
A lamp containing a gas or vapour that glows with light when an electric current passes through it. Mercury, neon and sodium vapour lamps produce strongly coloured light, but the light from fluorescent tubes approximates more closely to daylight.

Index

Acknowledgements

Picture Credits
Abbreviations used are: t top; c centre; b bottom; l left; r right.
Michael Freeman, the consultant photographer for this volume, is abbreviated as MF, John Garrett as JG and Image Bank as IB.

Cover: M. Garff/Image Bank

Title David Fairman. **7** Graeme Harris. **8-9** JG. **10** Ian Miles/IB. **10-11** JG. **12** Franco Fontana/IB. **13** Linda Burgess. **14-15** Robert Farber/IB. **15** John Sims. **16-17** Leo Mason. **18-19** Noble Beheler. **20** Paul Brierley. **21** MF. **22** MF. **23** tl tr bc MF, ct Ashvin Gatha, bl Sally & Richard Greenhill, br Jerry Young. **24** Roger Payling. **25** MF. **26** Linda Burgess. **27** tr Graeme Harris, l John Starr. **28** bl br Colin Molyneux/IB. **29** tl tr Linda Burgess, bl br Colin Molyneux/IB. **30** F C Gundlach/IB. **31** Peter Gittoes. **32** JG. **33** tl tr cl cr br JG, c Mari Mahr, bl Andrew Parkhouse. **34-35** Franco Fontana/IB. **36** Pete Turner/IB. **37** John Sims. **38** Mike Burgess. **39** t Cyril Isy-Schwart/IB, b Simon Yeo. **40-41** Vautier/de Nanxe. **41** t Vautier/de Nanxe, b Robin Laurance. **42** Ashvin Gatha. **42-43** Robin Laurance. **44** tr Brian Seed/Click/Chicago, bl Vautier/de Nanxe. **45** t Brian Seed/Click/Chicago, b Ashvin Gatha. **46** Linda Burgess. **47** t Pete Turner/IB, b Marcel Nauer. **48** tr Linda Burgess, b Ashvin Gatha. **49** Kate Salway. **50** David Parker. **51** t Linda Burgess, b Ashvin Gatha. **52** tr Jerry Young, b Peter Gittoes. **53** Robin Laurance. **54** tr Neill Menneer, bl Ashvin Gatha. **54-55** Franco Fontana/IB. **56-57** John Hedgecoe. **58** Pete Turner/IB. **58-59** Ashvin Gatha. **60** Graeme Harris. **61** t Linda Burgess, b Lisl Dennis/IB. **62** bl Walter Iooss/IB, cr JG. **63** Cecil Jospé. **64** Michelle Garrett. **65** t JG, b Linda Burgess. **66** MF. **67** Michael Borum/IB. **68** Alain Choisnet/IB. **69** tl Ian Bradshaw, tr Max Hess, b MF. **70** l MF, r Bill Plummer/IB. **71** Max Hess. **72** l Grafton Marshall Smith/IB, r G Palmer/IB. **73** t Franco Fontana/IB, b Frantz Thionville/Kodak. **74** tl Vautier/de Nanxe, tr Larry Dale Gordon/IB, b Wal R Gyr. **75** Ian McKinnell. **76** l Michelle Garrett, r JG. **77** t JG, b Niki Mareschal/IB. **78** l Donald E Carroll/IB, r Ellis Herwig/IB. **79** t Gerard Champlong/IB, b Vautier/de Nanxe. **80** Eberhard Grames. **80-81** Arthur D Arazien/IB. **82** tl Robin Laurance, tc Graeme Harris, tr André Chastel/Kodak, b John Hedgecoe. **83** Pete Turner/IB. **84-85** Dennis Stock/Magnum. **86** t Ian McKinnell, b John Sims. **87** Michel Casino/IB. **88** t Walter Rawlings, b Ernst Haas/Magnum. **88-89** G M Smith/IB. **90** Ian McKinnell. **91** J P Lescourret/fotogram. **92** Julian Calder. **92-93** Nadia Mackenzie. **94** t Franco Fontana/IB, bl Ian McKinnell, br MF. **95** Franco Fontana/IB. **96** l JG, c Geoff Nobes/Press-Tige Pictures, r MF. **97** Linda Burgess. **98** Pete Turner/IB. **99** Alain Choisnet/IB. **100** Jacques Alexandre/IB. **101** t Ralf Schutt, b John Sims.

Artists Kuo Kang Chen, Roy Flooks, Alan Suttie

Kodak, Ektachrome, Kodachrome and Kodacolor are trademarks

Printer by Printer Industria Gráfica S.A.
Provenza 388, Barcelona
Depósito legal B. 23385-1984
Printed in Spain